Roy
You are such
a Powerful Gift
to Humanity—
Shine Brightly
Love
Aunty Sandy
9-21-2019

When God Leads...
just follow

Written by
Sandy Rodgers

Sandy Rodgers

When God Leads...
just follow

Written by
Sandy Rodgers

WHEN GOD LEADS…just follow
By Sandy Rodgers

Library of Congress Catalog Card Number: 001-331-963
ISBN: 0-9723536-6-6
Copyright 2007 Sandy Rodgers
Updated 2011 Sandy Rodgers

All rights reserved. No part of this book may be reproduced by any mechanical, photographic or electronic process, or in the form of a phonographic recording nor may it be stored in a retrieval system, transmitted, or otherwise be copied for public or private use – other than for "fair use" as brief quotations embodied in articles and reviews – without prior written permission from the author.

Please address inquiries to:
Sandy Rodgers
P.O. Box 67
Austell, GA 30168

Editorial Consultants:
Marlo Oliver
Jae Duncan

Dedication

This book is lovingly dedicated to my son, Malcolm Jerome Tyson, who has consistently loved and urged me along this journey of life; always with words of wisdom from his young age of four. I thank you, son, for being my child, I LOVE YOU.

And to my Wonder-filled sister, Leah Janice Morrow, July 8, 1946 to April 12, 2010; my Sis lived an abundantly beautiful life, always following her inner urging, her heart. The heart is love energy, the heart is God! Thus the title: ***When God Leads… just follow***, is exemplary of Janice's entire life.

This is also dedicated to the Universe and each soul that is yearning to live out their purpose while residing here on Mother Earth.

Giving Gratitude

My sincere appreciation and unyielding gratitude goes out to the multitude that has supported me by constant prayer and Love. I can feel the power of the prayers that are being said on my behalf. Some of you have taken the time to express your love, while others are unable yet support me with prayer sometimes without my knowledge. I can feel it as I move through each day, the Prayer Power that keeps me moving forward.

To my parents I say thank you for joining together to create my existence. I truly love my life. Even during challenges, I am Thankful. Your love is always there and here, always with me. I know it and I trust it.

To my siblings, I appreciate the spice you add to our family recipe. What a delicious main course we are. Our children and grandchildren are the dessert, the sweet dishes of life. I thank you for a lifelong support system and your unconditional love.

To my beautiful grandchildren, Derrius and Deja, who keep me young, thinking and playful. Through the years as they have grown, so has the curiosity. Keep exploring, learning and loving. You are only limited by your thoughts of what you think is possible.

To my extended and worldwide family who has kept me held high during my human down time. I THANK GOD for you. You came at just the right time, the perfect time according to God's plan for my life. Some of you have been with me all my life and others are relatively new on my path. Irrespective of your time, our time, I appreciate you as my Perfect Present.

To my Spiritual Warriors and Angels, you know who you are. Thank you for your spirit, your strength and your wisdom.

To each person mentioned in this book, thank you for sharing a portion of your life with me. Thanks for being my teacher and student. Thank you for your presence, for I sincerely treasure you.

To the professional editing team, Jae Duncan and Marlo Oliver, thank you for maintaining the integrity of this writing. Thank you for your dedication to using your gifts to aide in this project.

Special appreciation to Joyce Mottley, for your graphic artist expertise and your wonderful friendship, and a business partnership that keeps expanding, you are wonderful. Thank you for your demonstration of Faith while facing and overcoming health challenges. You gave me strength by your actions.

Lastly to my James group – Timothy James Branch, James Lee McFarland, James Williams, Rev. James Suber, James Bailey (JB) and my father James Armstead. It is truly amazing to be surrounded by so many incredible individuals who all share the same name! I love you so much, a little bit of heaven is given to me by each one and I am Grateful.

Sandy Rodgers

Table of Contents

Dedication	5
Giving Gratitude	6
Preface	11
Introduction	13
1. Led by Angels, A Journey in Faith	17
2. Am I Sane?	31
3. Faith	37
4. Living Struggle Free	45
5. And the Beat Goes On	53
6. Are You Ready For Your Healing?	61
7. And Then There Was One	75
8. Healing Thoughts	85
9. My Journey to Ministry	93
10. Coming Full Circle	107
Conclusion	113
Listing of Websites	115
About Sandy	117

Sandy Rodgers

When God leads...just follow

God, Universal Spirit, The Creator, is that inner voice that whispers to you. That inner voice is intuition that tells you and reveals to you an urging to do something. It may come in a dream while you are sleeping or in a vision while you are wide awake. It may flash across your mind like a movie or as subtly as an infomercial. It may happen as you are caught in traffic on a highway or interstate. It may happen as you are intently listening to a speaker. However it comes to you, trust the process. It comes to you fully clothed and complete. All that is required of you is to trust it, trust yourself, and trust its infinite possibility. The Universe is waiting for you – to hush fear and proceed in faith; to silence hate and live in unconditional love. The Universe's only job is to support you and your wishes, i.e. your thoughts!

So often we dismiss the dream, our dream. We dismiss it mainly because we have stopped believing in our dreams. We have become robots, trained by a system(s) that does not honor our creativity. A system that strongly discourages individuality, a system that uses a vast diversity of mediums to create non-thinking, uncreative, robots! So it is no wonder we have stopped believing in our dreams, killed the inner genius of creativity. We are thought to be weird, different, non-conformist, labeled as a troublemaker, a misfit and the negative labels go on and on. Because the system is perfected on making sure we do not cross the line into our genius and original creative souls, we have accepted, without thought or consciousness, the very idea that kills our inner spirit.

God, Universal Spirit, The Creator speaks to each of us. No one person is any more privy to receiving this indwelling guidance. The Creator speaks to all – Pastors, Rabbis, and Imams, homeless, homosexuals, corporate leaders, unemployed, welfare recipients, adults and children. Our only task is to listen. Truly listen and take action. Faith requires action. Living your dreams require action. Living beyond mediocrity requires action.

We must unlearn the restrictions! Unlearn the conditionings that demand we believe we are unworthy individuals. We must unlearn the trappings of conformity. Each person is unique. Therefore your talents and gifts are different. They are different from your parents, siblings, significant other, friends or any others. Different from any other thought, idea or dream. You are the master and creator of your dreams. The Universe truly desires to manifest your dreams into reality. Are you bold enough to live your dreams?

So why go where God leads you? Why not? When each soul lives their destiny, fulfills their purpose, expresses their talents, how wonderful the kaleidoscope of manifested Dreams into Reality! How awesome and amazing the differences we each express. How glorious the Universe!

Introduction

It is my endowed gift to write in a plain language that the majority can understand. I accept that I am led to write and that it is my anointing to do so. It is an effortless task.

It is for you to read these simple stories which explain how you can be richly blessed by allowing yourself to easily go with the flow of life, so the next time (you have a hunch), you will instinctively know….

When God Leads….*just follow*

Years ago when I relocated to Atlanta from Los Angeles and wrote letters home to family and friends, the most repeated response from those receiving my letters was that they could <u>feel</u> themselves in Atlanta. I was told my writing was vivid and painted an exact picture which allowed the recipient to experience Atlanta while being somewhere else in the world.

At first I thought the encouragement was flattering and I enjoyed receiving the accolades. However, over the next several years, it became more and more clear to me that my writing was truly a creative gift, just as my clothing design had been a gift. I was highly encouraged to share my raw talent with others. With the kind words of my friends and family as my foundation, I was encouraged to write more and eventually decided to become an author of published works.

When God Leads…just follow

Over recent years, an increasing number of acquaintances have inquired about how and why I chose to move to Atlanta and do all the things I have with my life. Many have said that I have lived the life most people only dream about; that I have accomplished such a wide range of goals. They have asked me how I did what I did or what motivated me to never settle or become content; always choosing to do something so drastically different from what I had done before.

My response to them is simple: I have always felt a bit different from others, as a result, I did "my own thing". Most times I could not explain it nor did I want to. It was, and still is, exciting to me to learn new things. When an opportunity arose I always volunteered. I thrived on learning and doing something unique. I was seldom content and managed to multi-task most of my life.

In school, I refused to take courses that were regular or customary for girls, like typing. I resisted the standard rules and chose classes like Wood Shop and I absolutely loved it! I did not want to type. In my mind, I was not going to be a secretary, so why waste my time learning a typewriter keyboard?

In High School I designed and made my own clothing mainly because I enjoyed looking, and subsequently, feeling different. I remember being constantly asked, "Where did you get the idea to make that outfit?" My clothes were colorful, stylish and extremely original in design. I think it was just my desire to fully express my unique creativity. I perfected my talent of designing and sewing.

In December of 2006 I was told that I would be doing more writing. I had already written and published my first two books, *All My Men* and *The Rose Garden...remembering our beauty in tough times.* I was told I would have a bookstore with my name on it. I listened and accepted this spiritual inspiration from Mother Burks, delivered to me by her Godson, Timothy Branch.

Little did I know at the time how this would manifest in the physical realm. On January 1, 2007, I was filled with an abundance of gratitude for those who were actively participating in my life. With each bringing a unique contribution to me, I wrote each one a personalized note of Gratitude and emailed them.

The very next day I began writing daily messages. The first recipients probably numbered ten to fifteen people. Each day I wrote and sent them out over the internet. Within two months, my blessings are many and have prospered the lives of hundreds around the world. My direct contact list is up to two hundred and the people receiving the Daily IN-spirations are forwarding them to their family and friends.

I receive constant confirmation that I am allowing Spirit to guide and direct me. I am serving as a blessing to others, many of whom I do not know personally. The messages are universal, meaning it does not follow any particular doctrine or theology. I write about everyday human issues and concerns. The messages are for everyone.

What is so amazing is the lack of physical effort required on my part to write these messages. Most times I simply sit at the computer and position my fingers over the keys. Before I know it, I am finished with a beautifully inspired message. The days I feel that perhaps the message could have been stronger prove to be the days that I receive more notes of thanks from my readers. So, I know the messages are divinely IN-spired. All that is required of me is to allow my gift to be shared with others.

So, I have come to accept that this gift of writing is all about the *reader* of the messages. I understand that even if my ego mind tells me it could be or should be more, I send them out exactly as they were originally received and written. Often, I sit back in amazement by the multitudes the messages have helped with life challenges.

This is simply more confirmation for this particular writing. I have shared this book with several close friends and when I hear them quoting from this book or advising people how perfectly timed this book is, I am indeed humbled. I have heard statements such as, "That's why Sandy wrote her latest book." Or "That's exactly what Sandy said in her book" or "It's all included in the book, *When God Leads*".

So here it is just for you. My prayer is that this book richly blesses you and inspires you to do whatever it is that you truly desire to do. And even though you may be skeptical right now, go ahead and move forward, one step at a time, until you reach your desired destination, dream or goal.

Sit back, relax and enjoy stories of everyday, ordinary people doing extraordinary things with their lives because they know….

When God Leads…..just follow!

Chapter One

LED BY ANGELS – A JOURNEY IN FAITH

It all began one day in August, the summer of 1992, when Sandy was taking her three sons – Malcolm, Darryl and Chantz – on a trip to Atlanta, GA. Actually only one of the three, Malcolm, did she labor with for three days to give birth and bring a new life into this world. The other two had been adopted into Sandy's family, like so many others were. Malcolm was 16; Darryl was 17 and Chantz a mere 2 years old. Sandy's only birth son, a young 16 year old, black man-child was being escorted to attend Morehouse College some 3000 miles from where his family and roots were. This was indeed an awesome and exhilarating excursion for all four. All were excited to make this trip, it meant so much. This was the first airplane flight for both Darryl and Chantz.

Upon arrival to the airport in Atlanta, something strange and wonderful happened to all, but particularly for Sandy. Sandy had passed through Atlanta as a teenager herself many years before, but had not realized the beauty of this majestic, wondrous place. Atlanta had clean air, trees everywhere, picturesque scenery and displayed the glory of God's meticulous handiwork. Sandy knew immediately, that although she was indebted to her homeland in Los Angeles, she must relocate to Atlanta.

For the beauty in everyone they met and everything they saw had overtaken them all completely.

During Sandy's week long stay in Atlanta, she thought about her hectic schedule back home, working endless hours to make her business successful; a mortgage owed on a house that would now seem empty without her beloved son there; all the friends she had made and loved during her lifetime. The clubs and organizations she belonged to and was active in.

Her newfound Church home, FAME – First African Methodist Episcopal, a place that she cherished. Pastor Cecil Murray was the epitome of religious leaders. Pastor Murray always delivered a thought provoking and life changing message. It had been several years since Sandy was a part of a Spiritual movement such as FAME. The atmosphere was wonderful and full of praise and worship. Pastor Murray was joyous with a wide beaming smile each time you saw him. It seemed she had been searching for just the right Church where she could worship and serve the community and at long last it had been found.

In Los Angeles there were familiar places, surroundings known all too well because of a lifelong history living and growing up there. The weather in Los Angeles was enjoyed by everyone who lived there, seldom any extreme weather conditions to contend with, mostly warm the entire year. Close proximity to the beaches, a place she often went for reflection, solitude and inner peace. In Los Angeles you are only a short drive to the mountains or desert, this variety of venues is not necessarily available in other states.

But most important to Sandy, was the thought of leaving her family. A rather typical family in most regards, yet a very close knit and supportive unit of folks. Her family always garnered strength whenever a crisis arose within the family or with one of the family members. They expressed unconditional love; the underlying theme was whoever was the most appropriate member to handle a situation, that person did so without regard to whether it was their issue. A family nurtured by two sets of loving parents who sincerely loved all members. How could she think about abandoning all the comforts of a place called home, for this newfound frontier called Atlanta? But the thought of relocating would not go away; it was constantly on her mind.

On her return home, Sandy learned of devastating events that had taken place during her absence that almost ruined her business. This news shattered Sandy's spirit, which was always high and free flowing. The idea of relocating took a back burner position.

Almost lost in deep depression, isolation was Sandy's defense as she attempted to figure her next business move. To the rescue were her family, her Dad and her sister, Janice. They read scriptures to uplift her; they kept a vigilant watch over Sandy until she felt better.

The business was one in which she took enormous pride and had invested all of her retirement money and savings for its mere survival. Sandy was raised with the belief system that one should always give back to the community, to the youth, and that was what she was attempting to accomplish.

With that belief so deeply ingrained in the very fiber of her soul, she owned and operated a Youth Performing Arts Center in South Central Los Angeles. Nu Vision Modeling and Entertainment Inc. offered programs to children who would not have been exposed to otherwise. For their positive experiences in life were few, if any.

Sandy believed in the inherent God given talents of individuals but particularly the children. The children and parents alike loved Sandy, for she loved them, and it showed in all of her actions.

The house was surely empty. Malcolm was missed tremendously but the anticipated rewards from his education at Morehouse College made it all worthwhile. Even the dog felt the emptiness in the house. It was as if Cody had emotions also. Cody would mope around on some days not being his normal extremely playful self. Cody, an Akita, was huge and could put its paws on Sandy's shoulders when he stood up.

The weather was hot and Sandy often left the sliding glass door in her bedroom opened at night. Cody would be right there to protect her, guarding her all night long. If she moved so did Cody.

Sandy had looked for a roommate but her search was unsuccessful. The house was spacious with plenty of play area in the back yard. The house had been remodeled years earlier as a family project by Sandy's supportive family business, Brown and Brown Construction. The family business had completed the renovations in such a quality that it was definitely a house for children, with plenty of room and space.

After careful consideration, she decided to move out of the house and rent it to a large family. Several families were interviewed. The family that finally took the house as their home had six small children, which included the couples' grandchildren as well as their own children. Each month when Sandy collected the rent all the children would run to her and find a place on her small body to cling to. Neither runny noses nor soiled diapers affected the joyous occasions they enjoyed. Sometimes, the children would cry when Sandy left them.

Sandy had lived in this house for twelve years. She had neighbors she had grown to know and love, and had collected stuff – lots of stuff – during those twelve years.

The packing was a tremendous chore, but to the rescue were the packing Angels, better known as Sandy's closest friends.

It took days to pack and sort through everything and it was a successful move, Thanks to her Angels. Furniture was given away. Clothes were donated to charities. The Angels found their keep sake treasures while packing. And still a huge warehouse space was filled with the remaining items.

Little by little, all the ties that had kept Sandy from making that move to Atlanta were being broken. Also, Sandy was suffering from serious financial matters. The business that had been supported by her entire retirement and savings was being dissolved. The house was in foreclosure by the bank. Now it seemed all the financial planning she had done earlier in life was a joke, a bitter joke. Likewise, the love of her life made decisions about his future that did not include her as a main character.

After two years of pleading with his Mom, Malcolm finally persuaded Sandy to promise she would at last make that move to Atlanta. Malcolm had felt his Mother's pain even though she did not discuss it. She was a proud Black Woman who did not wallow in self-pity or blame her problems on some evil forces in the universe nor would she bow her head in defeat.

This was January, right after Malcolm had returned to school from his winter vacation in Los Angeles. Sandy promised to be in Atlanta by June 1st. So at long last the date had been set and the move was definitely on! Each was excited although Sandy's excitement was mixed with uncertainty.

The following month as Sandy was working as a salesperson at Circuit City in Lakewood California, her former Junior High School music teacher, whom she had not seen in more than thirty years walked into the very store where she worked. Mr. Persley was obviously excited to see Sandy. They recognized each other immediately, even though Sandy had lost a great deal of weight since her teen years. Mr. Persley made comments to Sandy about her weight loss, asking if she had been sick. He was always joking around. Then Mr. Persley had the whole store, sales people and customers laughing hysterically with his stories exaggerating how terrible Sandy was at learning to play the violin and cello. Mr. Persley invited Sandy and her sister to join him at his church on the following Sunday, he was going to be speaking. Sandy graciously accepted the invitation for them; they often attended church with Mr. Persley as teenagers. Mr. Persley was another example of sharing his life with the youth of the community. Sandy was filled with peace and faith as the congregation prayed with her about her impending decision to move to Atlanta. Instantly, Sandy knew the move was the right thing to do. It had been blessed by Christians, Believers of God!!!

Sandy carefully calculated the amount of money it would take to accomplish this move. The plan was put into motion, she cross-trained for a new department, and then another department in the store so that she could earn more money. She was now able to sell from three different departments. This plan of hers had to work, she couldn't break her promise to Malcolm nor did she want to. She was very confident of things working out financially.

She had five months to pay off her existing financial obligations and save for the expected expenses of the new apartment – rent, food and utilities. Plus she had loaned money to several people who would now repay their debt to her. Malcolm handled all the arrangements for their new living quarters in Atlanta.

Sandy kept meticulous records of moving expenses. She researched, checked and compared prices for moving vans and companies. After careful considerations and cost comparison she made her decision. She would have her belongings transported by a moving company that staggered collections across the U.S. of people's property to transport. It lowered the cost to stack several households on the same tractor trailer. She gathered her belongings from several family members' houses who had graciously allowed her storage space for her things. She began packing again. She remained in constant prayer.

By this time Sandy was sharing her widowed father's house with him. He did not want her to leave; after all she was his "Baby Girl" and was filling a void in his now empty house. He actually did not accept she was leaving until she started bringing boxes home from work for packing. Sandy's dad had really wanted to move back to his birthplace in Louisiana, especially after the death of his long time companion and wife. Dad simply changed his mind and decided to stay in Los Angeles. Sandy had told him months earlier, "Do not stay in Los Angeles because of me, I cannot promise this is where I will live for the rest of my life." On some level dad still wanted to move back to his birthplace and didn't. And by the time he had changed his mind again about relocating the property he had been secretly wanting to purchase had been recently sold.

The Manager of the store where Sandy now worked did not want her to go either, although he helped to arrange her transfer within the company to Atlanta. Sandy had become instrumental in changing the attitudes of the workers at the store. Now everyone spoke to each other and greeted each other with a smile.

The elderly customers genuinely loved Sandy and sought her out each time they made a purchase at the store. They loved her because Sandy never pressured them into buying anything or suggesting they purchase the most expensive items available. They often referred their friends to Sandy.

She always took time to carefully explain the instruction booklets, would re write them in plain language and ensured the customer could actually operate whatever they purchased. Sometimes this meant she went out to their residence for demonstrations, approved by the Store Manger of course.

She would write out the instructions in big letters on a single piece of paper and made sure the elder customer understood what was written before she left their residence. No one, either working in the store or who was a regular customer, wanted to see Sandy leave. The Manager, Dave Licht, and dad tried to work on a scheme to make her stay. Much to their dismay their scheme failed. To see the two of them devising their scheme was interesting. They never gave any considerations that Dad coming to the store all the time looked suspicious. They did their best.

Truly no one truly believed Sandy would leave neither her family nor friends. She had always been there for them. Always. Always ready to listen, to lend a helping hand, to baby-sit, to be a companion to the elder members of the family, enjoying dinner at Senior Citizen prices! Always there to joke and make their day a little brighter with her smile, which she always wore. Always ready, even if she did not get to go. A phrase her brother-in-law used to describe Sandy's attitude.

Finally the DAY everyone dreaded became a reality. The moving truck had been packed and was on its way to Atlanta with Sandy's household furnishings and personal goods. Janice, Sandy's sister, had offered to host the farewell party. Everyone joined in the decorating and preparations for the event. Banners put up, food cooked, music equipment set up, gifts bought, all the smallest of details were taken care of.

Sandy packed the few remaining things from her dad's house and headed for the last time, over to her sister's house. The drive seemed endless. The once familiar streets looked vaguely different to her now. But she knew it was still all good.

The grandest, most elaborate, and loving celebration of one's life was about to take place. Sandy arrived early; she wanted to spend as much time as possible with her sister, Janice, the one whose soul was so close to hers. Tears were fought off all afternoon; laughter was the main theme and order of the day. Well wishes and God's blessings. Presently, everyone accepted the move was definitely happening.

All the ANGELS from Sandy's life came. They came from all across the United States to bid a grand farewell to their beloved friend and family member. Friends from earliest childhood through the current time, which included new friends and old friends. Hundreds of people flocked to the celebration. Two ex-father-in-laws and their sons came. Teachers from Elementary, Junior and Senior High School attended. Co-workers from all the former jobs she had held. Students and youth from the many organizations she presided over were all present. As old as 90 years and as young as a few months all came. Black, White, Hispanic, Belizean, African, Native Americans. Teachers, counselors, nieces, nephews, sisters, brothers, aunts, uncles, cousins, former boy/man friends, friends of friends were all there. Business associates and business partners came. Many who had shared their lives with Sandy, felt the empty space her leaving would create, now starting to form.

Testimonies, two cakes, special surprise gifts, tears, dancing, a pure celebration of life! The invitation list included everyone past and present in Sandy's life – each with his or her own God uniqueness. Visual signs of hugs and affection filled the atmosphere. Folks mingled, the interaction between ages and ethnic groups was awesome. The gathering would make Martin Luther King Jr. know his dream was surely alive and well, peopled not judged by the color of their skin (nor age) but by the content of their character! Friends who had not seen each other since childhood were reunited. They shared their stories with each other, introduced mates, and showed pictures of their family. Former students expressed gratitude to their teachers who had contributed to their current success. The youngsters served as reminders to the older people, claiming their own piece of history as ambassadors of the future. The disbelief in Sandy's departure was a common thread woven between the strangers who were now well acquainted and new friends.

Cameras, lights, ACTION. Flashes from cameras blinded many. The jockeying for the best position with the camcorder took place. Everyone wanted a lasting memory of this once in a lifetime event.

Of the many well wishers with their unique individual support and prayers, there were certain incidents that Sandy will always hold dear in her heart of hearts. Dancing the swing with Mr. Thomas, an 80+ year old she had entered into several dance contests with in the past. They won several of the dance contests they entered. Mr. Thomas – a tall, slim, neat dresser – and Sandy loved dancing together and it showed in their graceful steps and the rhythm they shared. Everyone crowded around and cheered as they performed so elegantly.

Novelita, a cousin and kindred spirit, had been a constant companion of Sandy's during their teen years. She lived in San Francisco. Each summer they got the opportunity to fly on an airplane to visit. Novelita was paralyzed in a car accident at the tender age of 16. That did not stop their love for one another and the relationship continued. Novelita presented Sandy with a Butterfly pendant. She said it symbolized her flight of freedom and the beauty she has always had.

The pizza delivery! What a delightful surprise that was. Only those in attendance would understand, but all enjoyed. The crowd enjoyed making Sandy feel special and to see how she would react to such an unusual treat!

Dad made all the banners and a gigantic Bon Voyage card for everyone there to sign with their well wishes. A special song composed by her nephew, A.K., who just happens to be a well-known performing artist. Her two nieces, Juandessa and Nona, insisted no crying was allowed. They hid in the bathroom to cry their own tears. They didn't think Auntie Sandy would find out. Nona said, others often made fun of her dark skin tone and made her feel ugly, but not Auntie Sandy. Nona always loved her Auntie for that vote of confidence she instilled in her. Juandessa also known as Dee Dee looked like Sandy's twin sister. Dee Dee's mother, Janice and Sandy did not look like the sisters which they were. Dee Dee called on her Auntie often and would definitely have a tremendous void now in her life with her gone. Of course there was Big Brother George. Sandy respected her eldest brother's wisdom, love of life and his artistic creativity. Big Brother always loved his sister and had showered her with gifts, cards, support and encouragement all her life.

During her childhood Sandy always clung to her many Uncles with great care and respect. Only one Uncle was now still alive, Uncle Buddy. She had grown so close to him, they did a lot together and at one time Sandy lived with Uncle Buddy. They would talk for long periods of time and go out to lunch often. She almost did not leave because of the closeness and love they shared. Sandy's Aunts were there with plenty of love, words of wisdom and remembrances of their husbands. Mom simply said, "Just remember you can always come back home." The love was there, ever so present and alive. Mom squeezed Sandy so tightly every time they passed each other that night. There was no doubt to anyone that Mom would miss her 'Baby Girl' too.

    A money tree was there for anyone who wanted to make a cash gift to Sandy. At the start of the day Sandy didn't have the money to pay her rent when she arrived in Atlanta nor did she have traveling money for her long awaited journey. No gas money for the car, no money for food on the road, and no money for accommodations between Los Angeles and Atlanta. She would not and did not tell a single person, not even her family. Yet she still prepared to leave for Atlanta. All she knew was she was to make that move and she would stop at nothing less than that.

    Late into the night Sandy slipped away from the party, leaving her cherished family and friends to continue, so she could get the sleep she needed to start the cross country drive the next morning. Sandy was awake before the sun rose, as usual. She looked and all around her sister's house were sleeping bodies. There were people on the couch, floor, love seat and chairs.

    Sandy felt so loved. Something she had almost forgotten, either she had simply taken it for granted or hadn't felt that way in a long time. Scarred early in life with events she dare not even attempt to remember. Today, right now she knew that was all in her long lost past. All was very good right now. Thank GOD, for His Saving Grace and Loving-kindness.

As she sat feeling this tremendous love overcome her soul, she began to count the money that had been given the night before. Some people gave it in cards; some was placed in plain envelopes or was placed on the money tree, while others decided to give it directly to Sandy. Some of the people who gave, Sandy did not know, they were simply friends of friends or friends of family.

Sandy cried uncontrollably as she counted all that had been given to her. For now she had her rent money, grocery money, money to travel with and some extra spending cash besides. How she was to even make the trip without the physical evidence of cash never stopped her. She never gave strength to what appeared as lack of money substance. She stayed focused on her promise to her son that she would be there by June 1st. She glowed as she realized how much she was living her life in complete FAITH. How Blessed she was to have Angels in the human form of family and friends who cared and loved her so much!!

Sandy hugged her sister Janice, who would not get out of bed to say goodbye because it was much too painful for her to see her only sister leave. Who would go shopping with her now, who would listen to her tales about work and her daughters? No one could replace Sandy in her life. She was the one and only sister Janice had ever had. Sandy kissed the remaining folks in the house and said her goodbyes. Mom came to say bye, but all she could do was wish Sandy a safe and blessed journey. Dad was there to bless his daughter on her journey to a new home.

Years later, Sandy still cries tears of joy whenever she recounts the blessings of her life. Surely she has been

LED BY GOD. The decision and subsequent relocation to Atlanta was definitely – A JOURNEY IN FAITH.

Some times God uses Her humanity, people serving as Angels, as our guides. My Angels are God's human messengers. God can and does lead you by way of Angels on your life path.

The moral to this short story is **When God Leads and** you trust the process you <u>will</u> receive everything you require in divine order. Angels will appear to assist you in accomplishing that which God has placed in your heart. So go ahead with full abandonment of what you feel or see. Know without a doubt you are being led … and enjoy the journey!

Chapter Two

AM I SANE?

At one time or another, it may have even appeared to those around me that I had lost my senses. They were absolutely correct. I had lost my intellectual need at controlling, either situations or people. To be honest, I had no clue what else to do.

I had worked in the corporate world with Pacific Bell Telephone Company for twenty two (22) years when I heard my inner voice say, "It's time to go."

I had climbed the ladder and reached a very satisfying position. I was traveling the entire state of California in fulfilling my responsibilities as Statewide Resource Training Manager. I received numerous awards from the officers of the Company. The programs and training I developed were well received and implemented statewide. And I was earning a great salary with outstanding bonuses for the work I did.

In 1991 an opportunity for me to leave came forth. And I thought this was a very strange time for me to consider early retirement. My only child was a senior in high school and looking forward to going away to college, both requiring my financial contributions. I opted out with this early retirement program. However I had neither the age not length of service to qualify for immediate monthly payments. But, Spirit said to me "Go" and I did.

I founded Nu Vision Modeling and Entertainment Company within four months of my retirement! ***When God leads....just follow.***

I can recall times immediately following the Rodney King riots/unrest in Los Angeles. Our community was suffering a tremendous amount of trauma, just like with the Watts riots of the 60's. Months had passed and the smell, the awful stench of fire and devastation could still fill my nostrils.

Nu Vision Modeling and Entertainment Company was located on Vermont Avenue near Manchester Blvd. This was one of the major areas that were destroyed during this mass civil unrest. Buildings that formerly housed thriving businesses were completely destroyed by the raging fire that spread so quickly through our community. The effects still affect all my senses; I hear the screaming voices, I see the pandemonium of people in the street, I smell fire of burning buildings and I taste the smoke from the ashes.

The day the unrest burst forth was one of our regular class nights at Nu Vision. Nu Vision was dedicated to transforming lives of our young people in South Central Los Angeles. We had a huge positive impact on the hundreds we served. We produced role models through our programs. The program core principles were education and interpersonal skills. Nu Vision also instilled an attitude of "I Can" with all who graced our doors.

The company had begun with only 2 staff members and just 5 models. Yet we grew at an alarming rate to include models ranging in age form 2 to 92, Full Figured and Fine; men, women and children all benefited from Nu Vision. Programs expanded to include classes in drama, music, aerobics and other performing arts topics.

Nu Vision opened its doors to assisting businesses and offered space for them to begin. We conducted community related events that included an International Exchange Program with youth from Berlin Germany; weekly Men's Group meetings; Police and citizen meetings; we did whatever was necessary to enlarge our Community and the pride of its residents.

We held weekly round table discussions where all participated in open discussion about current events, community issues and personal development. This was particularly rewarding for the youth because they had a place where they could be heard in totality and where they were completely supported and encouraged by the adults of the company.

Many of our models rode the public bus to attend our classes. Time was of the essence due to the fast approaching and escalating danger of fire and the civil unrest. We hurriedly began making phone calls to instruct the students not to come. We were unsuccessful in reaching everyone so we, the staff, stayed until all were accounted for.

Many were unaware of the present dangers. Once we had all gathered in 'our' building, we formed a prayer circle and prayed. We prayed for everyone's safety in getting home and that 'our' building would be spared total destruction. We hugged each other, shared plenty of love with each other and departed.

Even living miles away did not lessen the noise of the helicopters overhead. You could see the blaze of the fire for miles. Too much devastation in one area! It appeared like some Hollywood movie, it was certainly unreal. Yet it wasn't some foreign country nor a make believe movie, it was indeed very, very real.

I made contact with everyone to confirm all had reached their destination and arrived home safely. Very early the next morning after a rather sleepless night, I headed to 'our' building. The Fire Department was still present. Smoke was slowly rising from the concert sidewalks and the streets, like steam from a tea kettle when the water has reached the boiling point. As I got closer I kept praying that all was well with my business neighbors and the local residents.

Getting even closer I noticed some buildings that were once standing were no longer visible! What a horrific sight! Smoke smoldering and just absolutely clinging and claiming the entire atmosphere, "Oh God, what has happened?" was the only thought recycling in my mind.

As a person who witnessed first hand the Watts riots of the 60's, it felt excruciatingly painful to drive down Vermont Avenue. Yet I had to go. I was the Director and it was my responsibility to the company. Worried that I probably should not get too close because everything still seemed to be hot! I finally located a safe parking space.

As I approached 'our' building I was numb. "Why is this happening?" I asked myself. Slowly I arrived, as if in a distorted slow motion, in front of 'our' building it was STILL STANDING!!! The Fire Department had cut into the metal gate that protected our belongings to verify no fire was burning inside. God had spared 'our' building!

The four adjacent businesses were burnt to the ground. Terrifying does not do justice to the suffering experienced. Large businesses, small businesses, livelihoods all lost – completely destroyed! Wow, wow, wow was all I could manage to say to myself.

It felt like a nightmare that I would soon awaken from. Maybe even a vision from a war torn area across the ocean, somewhere far away, but in fact it was our community.

So here we are, very close to Christmas. No neighborhood shops to purchase anything from, no local shopping available. The ugly sites of large heaps of cement and concrete from the destroyed buildings were all that remained. Vacant lots that once housed businesses, was now an ugly sight. Just plain old Ugly!

We did not want our children to suffer through the holidays. So with only two or three weeks I decided to host a Community Bazaar where local merchants could showcase and sell their wares. We also planned a Christmas party for 200 – 300 children. Our local businesses that survived the civil unrest of the Rodney King riot were asked to make donations of Christmas stockings, food, fruit, nuts and toys. We were told the usual request time is six months and so sorry we can't donate because it is a shorter timeframe than what is required. But those words did not stop Nu Vision Modeling and Entertainment.

We kept asking, often telling them before they could tell us what the required normal donation policy stated. We did not stop until every detail had been satisfied. I was told that we totally operated by Faith to host such a wonderfully successful event as the children enjoyed that year. Food, music, toys, filled Christmas stockings and a Santa! Everyone, especially the parents, appreciated the generosity extended to them.

That was a clear example of **When God Leads…. just follow**. We asked for what we wanted and received everything we asked for and more. The business people responded to our love and passion for the community and the children.

Sandy Rodgers

Chapter Three

FAITH

This morning my question going into meditation was "Why am I here?" The answer very clearly revealed itself to me, *"It's not about you (me) at all. It is about the lives you (I) touch!"*

My passion is in being of service to people. It does not matter the physical characteristics, young, old, male, female or color of the skin, economic status or religious belief or lack thereof.

I AM here to do God's work! I am here to promote Spiritual teachings and continue the work that my ancestors started. I am here to show mercy and understanding and to allow people to feel my compassion for them. To open my heart WIDE to receive what they have to say. To LISTEN without judgment or criticism. To be present in the moment with them!

So as I journey through this life experience I am reminded of the many times I have taken my hands off, simply surrendered; stepped way out in Faith. Truly not knowing the *why*, I said to myself 'Okay what do you do now?' All I really know is that I did not know. And this very space and place is where most people are, at least those honest enough to admit it. Another thing I know, without one single doubt is, whenever I admit to not knowing, that action opens the flood gates of wonderful blessings, allowing them to flow freely into my existence.

When God Leads, it can feel much like reckless abandonment of your well organized, goals oriented lifestyle. ***When God Leads***, you may and/or will feel like you have lost control of everything and simply you have. ***When God Leads***, your world appears to be spinning out of your control. And it is, Thanks God.

As a witness to allowing and accepting the power of God leading your life, miraculous events abundantly unfold in every area of your life. When you willingly release attachments to the outcomes, God can and will work everything out in Divine Order and Time. That's too simple, you now argue with me.

But how can I do that, you may ask? Especially when we have become so consumed, confused and accustomed to being led by ego. Start small, give one concern over to God. Give one day or even one hour to the Grace of God and just follow what you are being led to do.

Are you being told to release something? Or someone? How about being directed to mend a broken (separated) relationship? Are you being told to 'just be still and know I Am God'? Or dismiss all responsible actions and have some fun, for a change?

If you hear yourself saying, 'Oh NO! I can't do that!' that's your ego screaming to you. How can you even think about releasing worry about this tremendous obligation you are currently in? The writer is obviously delusional or at best some hyped up fanatical thinker. Doesn't the writer know nothing can get done or be resolved by <u>me</u> not <u>doing</u> something?

Even though I may not have a clue or I have spent countless hours, asleep and wake, figuring this out….and I am almost there! I smile with you because I have spent a great deal of my life caught, stuck in that place as well.

Rest and relax, Trust that inner feeling, the powerful voice of wisdom. Follow, without deviation or manipulation exactly what you are led to do. Watch the miracles unfold, better relationships, improved health, increased vitality, enriched financial gains and a more joyous you!

Marlo Brady Oliver is a Meditation Facilitator and the founder of Life After Breath, a holistic and wellness consultancy company. She is also my daughter, sister, mother, confidant, business associate and close friend.

She recently told of the circumstances of how she got started fulfilling her life purpose after one of her recent Dolphin Meditations. Marlo and I met a few years ago. The story as only she can tell it because its her story goes like this. It is a perfect example of how miracles happen **When God Leads**.

Marlo sat in the balcony one Sunday morning listening to Dr. Bertice Berry deliver a sermon at Hillside Chapel and Truth Center. Dr. Berry's theme was 'use your gifts or lose them'. Marlo said she thought about all the work she had learned to do by Breath Works and had not begun to do any of it. Dr. Berry's words pierced her heart of hearts. She made a decision at that moment to share her gifts with her church.

She began asking other church members that were standing in the hallways who she should talk to about her proposal. She was told 'Sandy Rodgers our Program Director'. Next Marlo needed to know who Sandy Rodgers was. So she went searching for me. It was not long before we were standing face to face in the Main Sanctuary. She explained why she wanted to talk with me and I said "Fine let's go to my office and we can set an appointment."

Per Marlo, she thought the process would be long and tedious. To the contrary I set an appointment with her the same day. Marlo said she was terrified to finally acknowledge her gifts and then ask to share them with others. It was done, the appointment had been set.

As Marlo arrived for her appointment, she was greeted by my normal embrace and huge smile. Once the door to the office was closed for privacy during our discussion Marlo broke down into tears. I just held her letting her know it was okay to cry. I did not know the reason behind the tears neither did I ask her to explain. We just sat until she was prepared to tell me about her proposal and her work. Marlo said "Sandy was so excited about my work. She said it was exactly what the church needed."

Marlo was assisted with all the support she required to launch her first meditation. I was so excited for her, always wanting to offer the opportunity for those who are prepared to share their gifts and talents.

Her first session was a huge success. Marlo has conducted Dolphin Meditations throughout Metropolitan Atlanta. She conducts group sessions and private one on one sessions.

What is so unique about this story is Marlo was telling it after our first collaborative effort combining her Dolphin Meditation with my Reiki skills. I am a Level II Reiki Practioner. The session was superb. Lots of healing manifested for the participants.

While away from home I had a vision of working in conjunction with Marlo. I was not sure what it would look like just knew we were to work together. Upon my return home I told Marlo of my vision. She simply laughed which she normally does when I say something that she has already experienced. She said she had the same vision while I was gone.

Today Marlo is a much sought after healer. She uses a variety of modalities in her healing work. She is taking classes at Ahimki Wellness Center with Dr. Mark Armstrong to obtain a degree in Naturopath Medicine.

She continues on her quest of learning as many different modalities of healing as she can. She calls forth the energy of the Ancestors and her perfect combination of skills and wisdom provides her clients with the best possible healing treatment. Her work has taken her to New Orleans Louisiana to help heal survivors of the Katrina Hurricane and to Alabama.

It's all because she answered her call. Marlo was frightened but worked through her fears and did what she was told to do. When God Led her, she followed. Her dream is now her reality!

Another example of a person allowing God to lead them is a good friend of mine, James Lee McFarland better known as Gentleman Jim. Gentleman Jim is a noted clothing designer extraordinaire. His designs and quality far surpasses most celebrated designers. His accomplishments have been noted in several publications, one naming him Atlanta's Best Designer!

Gentleman Jim has been in his craft for many, many years. He began in New York under the tutelage of Orie Wells, owner of Orie's Custom Tailoring. Their clientele included all the great names who either performed at The Apollo Theatre or were sports legends.

Gentleman Jim has owned several clothing shops in Atlanta, does custom tailoring, produced a sewing video, has show credits as custom designer for several stage plays and his list of accomplishments go on and on.

Jim had a vision of opening a Vintage Shop. He has recently graced Atlanta with his newest location called Van Miller. Although in itself this may not be very noteworthy other than he has seen his vision manifested. What makes his endeavor an answer to his prayer is that he has provided opportunities for several designers to showcase their unique creativity. In the shop one can find one of a kind designs by Gentleman Jim, vintage designs by Vanessa, corsets by Designer Cleah, leather accessories by Imana, and jewelry by California designer Lynette Hamilton.

When God Leads….just follow.

TV Anchor Darryl Hood grew up in Watts California. As a teenager, Darryl wanted to follow in the footsteps of KCAL's news personality Pat Harvey. Darryl was encouraged to write to Ms. Harvey for mentorship and guidance. He was encouraged to follow his dream.

Darryl wrote Ms. Harvey constantly with no response from her. I told Darryl he could do and be anything he chose. I also explained he should never give up if that was his dream. It was a very long time before he received any correspondence from Ms. Harvey. Darryl never gave up. He developed a relationship with Ms. Harvey and she agreed to mentor this eager and determined young man. As a result Darryl attended Northridge University with a major in broadcasting.

Darryl has been very successful in his career. While serving as the anchor for FOX5 in Las Vegas Nevada, Darryl was voted as one of Las Vegas' top bachelors. What was really exciting was to see his face on the sides of the buses in the city.

Darryl has enjoyed an awesome career in television. He has learned the industry all along the way. He desires to be able to teach other inner city youth in the future about broadcasting and the television industry.

Darryl followed his heart, his yearning, his desire. He never allowed fear or defeat to enter into his thinking. He always kept his sights on where he wanted to go. He serves as a role model for his younger siblings and others in the community.

When God Leads…just follow.

Sandy Rodgers

Chapter Four

LIVING STRUGGLE FREE

On a recent visit to Los Angeles, my physical birth place and birthing place, I had the rare opportunity to share with my two closest girlfriends from my adolescent years. Actually Criss and I went to kindergarten together before rejoining with each other in High School.

It was truly amazing to remember our lives together, lessons we learned, pains we shared, dreams lived and so on. And no wonder Candace's 36 year old twin daughters, La Saundra and La Shuan, wanted us to keep talking about our experiences. Each of us, Candace, Criss or myself remembered important events that sometimes the other couldn't. Thirty eight years since graduation and we sat and reminisced, recalling names of classmates like we had just left high school. Remembering things we had done that we hoped no one would ever find out about. It was simply incredible to be in their presence again. I felt like a little girl. Telling and sharing our truth, knowing the others would not understand us.

What we shared and talked about was the time of innocence; the time when others in your life just accepted you for who you are, without pretense. We all have had these experiences yet sometimes we lose contact with the very people who helped us along the way, the people who were designed to be an integral part of our make up. For us it was sisters sharing in strength, standing tall together in love. So it is no wonder that reuniting with these two girlfriends would fill my cup full of Thanksgiving. My cup runneth over.

This trip was more than just reconnecting with these two wonderful sisters. It was a trip I will always remember.

In preparing for this trip to Los Angeles, as usual I had a written agenda of activities. Mostly work related meetings were scheduled. I planned my time spent with my elders. They were always the first on my list of things to-do. Upon arrival into Los Angeles I would visit with the elders of my family and extended family, before doing anything else.

This trip was different, as my life was now more open to receiving and following the guidance of God. The blessings would be greater than anything I could have designed. I shared love with so many that it was awesome just to know that that many truly loved and cared for me. Putting this in a more meaningful way, I allowed people to express their love to me.

I had been a giver for so long it had become second nature for me to give. My problem existed with being a receiver. Someone once shared with me that in order to give someone must be in a receiving mode. I had never thought of it in that way before that was said to me.

It was always more comfortable for me to give, because that was what I chose to do. So this time in Los Angeles was spent in receiving monstrous love and affection. It was grand!

I spent quality time with elders ranging in age from 99 to 65; I am not always sure about the ages. Sometimes these tender folks just will not tell you the truth about their age! The wisdom they depart is like a well of knowledge, never ending. They will tell you about history from a very real perspective and not what you read in a history book. So I always like to ask questions and see their faces light up when they open up and start to tell you about the real deal. How absolutely incredible it is to hear them, you become a part of their past. They describe situations and events in such detail there is nothing left out of the story. Many in my family and in other families do not understand the wisdom and soul of our old folks. I cherish it, always have.

As a child when we would visit with our family in Louisiana I would want to sit with my elders, my uncles so they could tell me stories. I was always fascinated by them. And they knew I would be there to listen. I think sometimes they made up stories just to have something to tell me. It did not matter to me, as long as I could sit and listen. This lifelong habit of mine still continues as I visit with the elders.

These are my current elders – Uncle Buddy, Ms. Rose Jackson, Auth Ruth Moore, Ms. Leola Reed, Mr. Marcus Tyson, Mrs. Juanita Tyson, Mrs. Nellie Westbrook, Mr. Elihu Rodgers "Pops" and Mrs. Bernadine Rodgers "Mom". And they look for me when they know I am coming into town.

Uncle Buddy and I had our very special time together. I took him on several errands and made sure he was well satisfied.

I sat in the garden with the Tysons and was engaged in some rather tantalizing discussion with Mr. Tyson. Mr. Tyson loves to talk and I engage him in conversation with an attentive ear.

Ms. Jackson just wanted to get away from the nursing home for awhile. Ms. Jackson had begun to write the story of her life and was anxious to share her book with me.

Aunt Ruth spoke with such detail and clarity no one would ever figure out she is 99 years young! Aunt Ruth was living in her own apartment in an assisted living center that truly cared for the residents.

Pops told me he was now 8 zero, meaning he had just turned eighty. I thought it was cute and so did he. Not everyone agreed with us though. Pops and I had our vey own language and everyone respected that.

Mom was more alert than my last visit. She was taking less prescription medicines than before.

Ms. Leola always cast her love on me with great care and this was no exception. She is a delightful woman whom has become my other mother. Ms. Leola treated me to breakfast at one of her favorite restaurants in Long Beach.

Ms. Nellie and her sister Maud needed help with switching to a new remote for the TV. This is love in its purest form.

The love of the elders is so awesome. They have reached a point in life where they do not pretend about their feelings, they tell it like it is. And I guess most people do not want to know just how they feel about them. Getting the wisdom is easier when the elders are still with us.

I had gone to Los Angeles to participate as the featured speaker for the 3rd Annual Phenomenal Woman Appreciation Luncheon. In this time of sharing with these incredible women I knew I was fulfilling my purpose of living. I could see the eyes and souls of the eighty plus women in attendance. Everyone participated in the activities, even the younger girls. There were tears of joy and sorrow, sharing of hurts and disappointments, hope and honor, all giving and supporting each female in attendance.

All committed to a positive change and to report next year how they stretched during the year to create and bring about peace and a higher conscious way of living.

One elder was able to share her pain of her son's death about twenty years earlier and she asked me for help. I was honored to offer advice and comfort to this mother. There were sincere connections made between women of all backgrounds. When I was told by a most beloved elder and mentor that I delivered my message to the women with grace and full knowledge I knew I was in the right place at the right time. I had made an impact on these lives, a positive impact! Thanks God. **When God Leads**....

The comments shared about my presentation:
- Like the passion of breast feeding a baby. Soothing and nourishing to the soul of both the mother and child.
- Like giving water to a thirsty traveler.
- Giving food to a malnourished individual some got strength immediately while others received it more slowly.
- Some were digesting the thoughts presented many days later.

My family enjoyed, I mean really enjoyed time together on Mother's Day. Unlike any other time, there was more displayed love and acceptance of each person. Couples huddled together on the swing. Elders and younger folks talking, playing and laughing with each other, and children serving food to their elders. Older children were helping with the younger ones. Reconnecting and bonding with my peoples felt extremely good to me.

I allowed and accepted others loving me. I received it thoroughly in grace and humility! I received all the unconditional love others chose to give to me. I fully cherished each moment and kind act. I embraced everyone I encountered, felt their warmth and affection. Had it not been for me listening and obeying the 'voice' I would have missed this quality time with my family and friends. I had been so accustomed to living by an agenda of things to do. Rushing around to see everyone and to do as much as possible within the short time I would be visiting. What I required was this new energy shift. I left Los Angeles re-energized, renewed and revitalized. And that was a rare and new present to myself.

The gifts I received were spending an evening with a couple just watching TV and being fed as much catfish as I could eat. I almost felt embarrassed because I ate so much. Then I was reminded that it was prepared for me and with that being said I continued until I was stuffed. And the fish was delicious!

I hung out with my nieces and nephews at a motorcycle club. This was awesome because I used to hang out just like them. My ex husband and I were closely associated with members of several motorcycle clubs back in our day. I loved riding on the motorcycle. I loved the smell of fresh air. I loved not being enclosed in a vehicle. I loved the freedom riding on the back of a bike can give you. So to be included with them was so incredibly wonderful.

I was gifted with being a guest at a live cable television taping with my god-son. This was my first experience of watching the complete taping including all the cuts, retakes and deletions. The crew was so nervous of me watching that they were making all kinds of simple mistakes. I was so tickled as they kept repeating, 'Cut - Let's redo it!' I knew they wanted to impress me and that humbled me. My god-son and I had Sushi for lunch. What a treat, I go to Los Angeles and end up eating Sushi in Little Tokyo.

I visited with both of my ex husbands. They are each exceptional men. So to visit with them in a friendly and supportive atmosphere is very special to me. We began as friends and even if the marriage did not work, we should be able to maintain a friendship. And so I did and have been able to do just that. These two are gifts to me, gifts that I truly cherish.

This chapter is about allowing more love to come into your life; to truly enjoy your elders and your family; to reconnect with friends of your past; to just be more you in the present moment. Sometimes God just wants us to be. Accept the love of those around you in ways you never thought possible. You are truly worthy of the love.

I believe God will lead you into situations that are incredible and miraculous, all for you to see that miracles do and can happen all the time. You and I only need to be in a receptive state to enjoy the blessings enfolded into the many situations we find ourselves in.

When God Leads, it may be a friend, it may be a neighbor, it's possible for it to be that person you always pass without speaking, God may be leading you to a higher form of living that you have never experienced before. Be prepared to go there, just follow and see the blessings.

Sandy Rodgers

Chapter Five

AND THE BEAT GOES ON…SERENADING THE SPIRIT

When God leads you, you will be pushed gently past your current level of comfort. It's a place I like to call 'a zone of endless possibilities'. We place and sometimes force limitations of what we can achieve, what we allow ourselves to believe and who we can become. We operate inside "the box." Surely the underlying reasons why we limit ourselves are as numerous as the stars in the sky. Surely each of us has certain reasons why we limit ourselves. Yet we dare not admit it to ourselves or anyone else. "The box" is nothing more than an imaginary container that supports our limited thinking.

God plants the thought, the idea, the vision within us. Most times, if not each time, we ask "where did that come from?" If you are still in denial or insist that you do not have any thoughts, let me give you an example. This is one of mine.

Early one winter morning, I was in the midst of my regular routine. I sat on the ledge of my fireplace, drinking/sipping on some very delicious, steamy, hot coffee. I really enjoy the smell and taste of fresh brewed coffee. As I sat slowly enjoying each sip, a quiet voice spoke to me instructing me 'to write a song.' Well that was hilarious to me. Although for years I had believed I could not sing, carry a musical note, at one time I even sang Soprano as the lead singer in a church choir! More on that later.

Back to this wintry morning. My audible reply to the instruction was, 'Yeah, right!' So I continued drinking my rather delicious coffee. The voice got louder, "Sandy, write the music." Still I chose to ignore it, arguing that I did not know how and had never written a song before in my life. I was doing a great job in convincing myself that I lacked the skills and talent to complete such a task. I talked myself out of doing it without the benefit of ever attempting to do it. I was exhausted finding reasons why I could not write the songs. I continued drinking my coffee.

Suddenly that still small voice became a loud, loud "WRITE THE SONG." At this time I was simply tired of arguing. Yes, sometimes I argue with 'the voice'. However I usually do what 'the voice' tells me to do. And I figured I could prove to 'the voice' that I could not do it! So I said very loudly "OKAY ALREADY. I WILL DO IT!" It's a good thing I lived by myself at the time. So I got up and picked up a tablet and ink pen. Feeling deep inside of me, this would never manifest into anything tangible, but that I had to do it. You see, along this journey of life I have learned to follow this intuitive feeling.
Before I realized I had done it, I had written my very first song!!! And for the next several days I actually wrote seven songs total! I was elated, very excited. Then I felt so confused. Now what do I do with this, my songs? For surely 'the voice' knows I do not sing.

Oh that's right let me explain my singing experiences. Back some twenty years or so ago, I was a member of Disciples of Christ Church in Lynwood California. It was a very small congregation, I mean very small. The Pastor, Dr. V. J. Edner, hired an extremely talented composer and director, Mr. Raymond Rasberry, to work with the choir. Keep in mind the congregation was very small, maybe twenty total, including the Pastor. Mr. Rasberry was a personal friend of Pastor Edner. Mr. Rasberry asked me to join the choir. I laughed so hard. But you know I do not remember when I was told I could not sing. Whenever it was and whomever it was that told me, I thoroughly accepted it as my truth.

Mr. Rasberry didn't believe I couldn't sing or if he did he never acted like it. To me my voice is very deep, so I knew I would probably sing bass. When Mr. Rasberry asked me to sing these different notes, I thought 'Oh whatever, at least I am trying.' He finally decided I would sing Soprano! Now that was the exact moment I questioned Mr. Rasberry's musical talent and rationale. He insisted I could and would do it. Such confidence he displayed in me.

Weeks of rehearsal! Weeks of torture! Weeks of stretching way beyond my belief system of what I thought I could do.

The choir was now ready to perform. There I was, out in front singing the lead as a Soprano! No one was in more shock than me. The song was beautiful, I was beautiful. I could and I did!

Mr. Rasberry had more confidence in me than I had for myself. Sometimes we are blessed with angels on our journey to guide us past our own belief system.

But that singing talent did not last long and I returned to thinking, believing and affirming to myself and the Universe that I could not sing. And yes you are right, my notes are now off key. To remember this story is like a slap in my face, a reality check. Right now, I am thinking about all the talents I may have that are unexpressed because of someone else's opinion of me.

So here I am with an original song, *"A Beautiful Rose"*. I had typed it up on the computer. I was so excited, I immediately called my girlfriend Jae Duncan, a.k.a. JaStar. Jae is a melodic jazz songbird. She told me to send her the lyrics and she would take a look at them. Jae said she would work on the melody and call me later.

It was approaching the time to leave for work. I kept laughing to myself. All day long I thought about the events of the morning, The Voice, the instruction, then actually obeying and having a finished product!

Later that night Jae called very excited about what had happened to her. Jae said she could not think of a melody. She became frustrated and decided to just let it go. So she prepared herself for bed.

As she did she remembered a practice that she had used in the past that had worked. She put the printed words under her pillow, so that she would sleep on them for the night. She went back to the bathroom and said "Okay God, you gave Sandy the words, now I need the melody." When she crossed the threshold of her bedroom, the melody came complete to her. She recorded it on tape and called me. After explaining to me what had just occurred, she sung the song. It was indeed beautiful, it was perfect. God was truly using both of us in this.

JaStar mesmerized the audience as she performed her rendition of *"A Beautiful Rose"* at a Women's gathering at Hillside Chapel and Truth Center in Atlanta. She was absolutely fabulous as she sang a cappella. She received a standing ovation from the ladies.

The song touched the hearts of all those present! Jae told the group the history behind the song. The story alone is sufficient evidence of God working through people. Combine that with a finished product such as beautiful music then it becomes a Blessing to the listener.

"*A Beautiful Rose*" describes the life journey of women, the changing seasons, the pulling of weeds in the garden of life and so on. Each woman related to the story, the triumphs, the lessons and the full expression of women.

Then more songs came through me. Seven songs, one after another with wonderful messages flowed through me. I just kept writing as the words, the messages came. I could hardly believe what was happening.

Then another snag, what about the other songs? Oh that's right my nephew A.K., Anthony King, is a songwriter and producer. A.K. is self taught and exceptional, brilliant in every sense of the word, a musical genius! I was flying high. I called A.K. and left a message. Days passed and no return call, weeks passed with the same result. A month passed and still no phone call from A.K. I thought that perhaps I had an incorrect number for him. I called my niece and verified the number I had was correct. Okay I will call him again. A.K. and I always enjoyed a fabulous connection, very spiritual and extremely supportive.

When I phoned this time he answered. After about an hour of updating each other on our lives I told him about the songs I had written. A.K. said, "Okay Auntie, just email them to me." I told him I didn't know what the next move was and he directed me to read Exodus 31:1-10 in the Bible. After reading it, he explained to me that I had done what God directed me to do, now the Universe was able to complete the rest.

Two days later A.K. called full of life and enthusiasm. He sang his version of '*The Power*'. He had done a superb job! I loved it! But I did not and could not hear the pure composition because we were dealing with transmission via a cell phone. Yet he was so extremely excited. I loved what I heard, he insisted it sounded better.

He asked me for the melody of the next song, *'Inside of Me'*. I did not know and told him I trusted his creative ability and would leave it to him and Spirit because that was what I trusted the most with this project.

Within a few days he had completed three songs and shipped them overnight to me. The music was phenomenal. I was impressed, completely giggly and elated! A.K. was right, they sounded incredibly different and better than what I heard over the phone.

After finishing the third song, *"I Don't Wish No More"*, A.K. admitted several things to me. First was the fact he hadn't done any music in several years. He had put it to the side to pursue other interests. He agreed to do it for me because he was honored that I had called and asked him to do it. Another revelation was as A.K. put it, No one had ever, ever just sent him words on a piece of paper and called it a song!!! I laughed so hard because I did not know any better. It's a good thing too, because if I would have known I needed to do something else with it before sending to him, it would not have gotten done.

This joint project produced three incredible songs, with more to come. Each song with a very different beat has served as a healing balm for all who have heard them. Now to get these songs marketed to the Universe.

Its incredible how this all turned out, because the creative genius was re-awakened in A.K., he soon realized new thoughts flooding him. He began to see and hear from old friends who are also musically talented, he said he had not communicated with them in a long time.

We bonded again on a deeper, spiritual level. The music, the songs were healing for both of us. The music is a blessing because the messages are positive and life affirming. We each have our favorite song and sometimes that change as well depending on what is happening in our lives. Each song has an awesome beat! Stay tuned and check your local music outlet for this incredible music.

When God Leads…just follow

Sandy Rodgers

Chapter Six

ARE YOU READY FOR YOUR HEALING?

People can show up in your life to help you heal another relationship, perhaps a primary relationship. They can come into your life as friends or a significant other. Either way they come as earthly angels to guide us through our life experiences.

For example, an older woman befriends a younger female. It resembles a mother and daughter relationship due to the age difference. If both are of a higher consciousness both can heal if both are in need of healing. They can be the person who represents the challenge that requires healing.

If both have unresolved or partially resolved mother-daughter challenges, they can role play either or both parts. They each have the opportunity to love unconditionally, to nurture, to protect, to offer words of comfort and support. Each can embrace the other with arms of Love and Wisdom. Either can gently rock the other in a cradle of love, as a mother would with an infant child, singing a song or stroking the person's body.

And as this relationship develops, healing can occur. This is not to suggest or recommend one should seek out this type of friendship for the sole purpose of healing the past. Rather it is to say as you value yourself and the other person, fully loving each other unconditionally; you can reap other benefits also. You must grow the relationship with trust and love. Anything less is unacceptable.

God may also lead you away from a relationship, situation or employment. In our fear based consciousness we may attempt to ignore the instruction and stay where we are most comfortable, even if in that comfort zone is pain. We stay because it's familiar. We remain because we cannot see any other way or we have accepted lack as our reality.

When God leads, maybe you need to heal a relationship. I am elated to say that was my instructions. Was I surprised? Not at all. Because my work is in facilitating the healing of myself and others by whatever means necessary. So for me to satisfactorily fulfill my life's work then I must first do my healing work. As difficult as that could seem, the fact that I still had unresolved issues urged me to dig deeper. I was determined to search the crevices of my heart and soul to find where I still required healing. I was led to be completely honest with myself. It's comical however how well we can justify our own victim hood.

The mother daughter relationship sometimes has a very peculiar feel to it. I have discussed this phenomenon with sisters of all backgrounds the majority of my adult life. There's something magical about this relationship. There is also a powerful force that causes a deep separation of the two souls. Both withhold pure communication. Some ache for the love they secretly feel they deserve but are not receiving. A few act out that which they cannot verbally describe or explain. And for some the hidden hurts in their hearts have manifested themselves in very unhealthy ways. Either or both may harbor feelings of being unlovable or unworthy to receive love.

I have female/sister friends whose mothers were absent emotionally and/or physically. Women/Sisters who did not know the identity of their birthmother until they were adults or at best teenagers. Sisters who battle with the pain they feel regarding their mother. Mothers who secretly wish they could have handled the relationship with their daughter differently. Mothers who wish they could have shown more love, given more unconditional love, who could have shared honestly about life and being a female. In the hearts of these women there exist a gigantic hole, a true disconnect of their spirit.

The female energy is by nature, the nurturing element in the Universe. So when that energy is not at peace or not balanced it creates challenges in the core unit, the family. If it goes unchecked and unresolved it may create many generations of concealed/unresolved pain.

Those emotions can only be denied but for so long before a person will likely implode/explode from the weight of these burdens. Perhaps it will take two generations or maybe as much as five generations. Yet at some point the emotions must totally be addressed and resolved.

So today I sit and wonder where in my family history separation of Spirit occurred for the females. My mother recently shared with me that her grandmother died when she gave birth to her mother. So the community of women and her father raised her mother. So I wonder if that's where it began; the wounded-ness of my grandmother, my mother's mother not having her mother alive to nurture her as a child. Or maybe it goes back farther than this.

In 2004 I journeyed to Ghana West Africa. The sensation I felt in my body is beyond a verbal description. I was in the Motherland and joyously placed my feet in the sand on the beach and in the Atlantic Ocean. However my discovery of the beauty of being in Africa would also include a visit to the slave dungeons.

As I stood in the female dungeons in the Elmina Castle, the energies, the presence, the essence of the females that were held captive there penetrated my entire being. My body trembled as I experienced the dreadful experiences inflicted upon my ancestors.

Beginning with my feet of understanding to the crown of my head, I felt them. I felt the beauty, the royalty, their majestic essence. I felt the horror, the suffering, the pain and the humiliation. I felt their loss. I felt the shame of being physically raped by the captors. I heard their cries and the prayers. I felt the strength of these beautiful women, young and old. I sensed the robbing of their innocence; the pure violation of their souls.

All I could do was stand up for them, to acknowledge their torture, to be a witness for them. I was so ever present in that moment; it was life changing for me. What pain I felt. I still feel it, for I am forever connected to that energy. I will always remember that moment in time. I am grateful for the journey, for that experience.

I stood in that sacred space, with all the women who had traveled through this place. I was completely captivated by what I felt in that very moment. However that moment represented hundreds of years and thousands of females.

This moment was for me the beginning of my life. In that moment I accepted my role and responsibility for a global healing. For now I fully understood it was much larger than me, my family, my community or my country. I was in the Motherland feeling the vibrational energies of my fore mothers. The energy I felt was so real.

I transcended the current time and traveled back to a place that is still very real. A place still requiring healing of the pains that were afflicted on these, our own fore mothers. A place that cries out, begging for someone to hear and assist with the healing of the trauma that took place there. A place far away and yet very close; a place that is beckoning for assistance of the global healing that must take place.

The tour guide apologized for Africa's action that aided with the slave trade. How incredible that was to know that we each must accept responsibility when errors occur.

Could this be the point of disconnect?

Unknowing, on a conscious level, that that experience would spark a curiosity that would effect healing, God led me to that special place so that I could fulfill my life purpose. The Elmina Slave Dungeon was excruciatingly painful and joyously exhilarating at the same time. I shed so many tears, not all were of sorrow. The tears have served to propel me into a quest for healing of the feminine energy, globally.

Dr. Vanessa McAdams-Mahmoud of Mandala Psychotherapy Associates is a friend of mine. I met Dr. Vanessa just a few years ago. We were both presenters at a Women's conference. More than a year later we met again at a meeting of Black Social Workers. Dr. Vanessa invited me to her office to discuss the work she was completing.

It was very interesting to learn that her work dealt with the effects of unresolved emotional trauma – four generations later! I was indeed intrigued by the work. The visit to her office was very rewarding and opened my heart wider to healing. I was reminded of how the energy of our ancestors can and will affect us. I thoroughly appreciated Dr. Vanessa's work.

What a powerful calling for her to do this project. I am truly blessed to know this awesome woman. I was so honored that she would share her work with me. How awesome that God placed me in her life at this time. Now I have this information tucked inside my heart.

Then there's my dear friend, Dr. Pamelaia Sanders, Ph.D. (c), Transformative Learning and Change; founder of SpunKey Learning Concepts Inc. She is doing her dissertation work on The Resurgence of the Soul's Inner Well Spring of Knowledge, healing soul unrest in the Black Community.

She defines her work, Soul Unrest as disconnection from our divine, creative and cultural nature. This is actually Dr. Sanders' life work. She understands the impact of a nation, a world of unresolved issues has on the global situation of peace.

The incredible individuals on my path doing ascension work keeps growing; Tim Branch, Raja Crumbly, Joyce Mottley, Marlo Brady Oliver, Linda Samuel, Linda LA Boyd and Phyllis Austin, in the form of sincere friendships.

This ascension work is not new. Perhaps the terminology is new but not the work. My brother William and I discussed a few years ago the climate we were living in and the need for humanity to rise to a higher level of consciousness and being. We actually have been doing this work since the early 1960's. At varying degrees of completion and fully reactivated our thoughts and actions in 2001. This work is very timely. We are each able to ascend but few answer the call.

The works of author and columnist Karen Bishop, What's Up On Planet Earth, writes in detail about this awesome process. Her writings are filled with such compassion. She is truly in her perfect place and is a being on target.

Lisa Iverson, Family Constellations, facilitates sacred circles of healing. Family Constellations originated in Germany to aide in the healing of the emotional trauma experienced by holocaust survivors.

The work developed by Bert Hellinger of Germany utilizes the energy of the ancestors to reveal what needs to be resolved, "families have an invisible Blueprint that travels across generations. We are deeply bonded to family members we may not have ever known. These powerful forces guide and influence our lives", these are the quotes from the work of Family Constellations.

Raja Crumbly is one of my newest life friends. We met by referral of a third person, Mother Sharon. During our initial interaction of four hours, our main objective was to discover and disclose who we are. We began with the customary what we did, what we thought and what were our goals and dreams in life. We bonded instantly, like old friend reuniting. Raja is keenly spiritual and highly intellectual.

Raja's work focuses on helping people to heal. His specialty is his series, "The Elimination of Fear". This program is incredible in identifying the causes of fear and how to eradicate it forever from one's existence. The work is powerful just like its creator.

Raja honored me with the playing of his music. It is so pure and healing, the words and melodies are soothing to the soul. Somewhere during our deep and lengthy conversation, we began discussing our childhoods.

As I understand life, we each have the same story just with different character names. So it was no wonder that I opened up and discussed my relationship with my mother. Raja provided me with invaluable information that has made a huge impact on how I relate to my mother.

We explored the relationship in detail, the particular roles that my mother and I came to play in this life time. What each was to teach and learn from the other. It all made so much sense once I received clarity around our roles. I have used this information as a tool with my healing and communication with my mother.

This is what God meant when my soul was whispered to, to be still and know. There was no action required of me to search out these individuals. The Universe had worked this all out. Holy Spirit had aligned all the energies and resources that are required for healing. We must be alert and aware of their presence as they appear. We must be present in every moment to recognize the blessings as they occur. We have and use our faith, knowing everything is working out in Divine Order and Divine Time. We only need to walk out standing tall accepting the manifestation is perfectly aligned with the true desires of our hearts.

So for the past several years as I facilitate sessions on healing throughout the Universe I truly understand that the healing is always for me or you. And not the other person! WOW. What a concept. Praying for others is wonderful but communicating with God for yourself is the best thing you can do. Indeed, it is only yourself that you can effectively change. And the change that is necessary is in your thoughts.

As soon as you open yourself up to accepting a different reality, one based solidly in Truth, situations begin to present themselves to you to support your new thoughts. For me this manifested as a more loving relationship with my mother. I chose to think a new thought. Perhaps what I held as reality was not real at all.

After experiencing many years of a disconnect, I am extremely grateful to say I am currently sharing a renewed relationship with my mother. A relationship filled with unconditional love, respect, wisdom and understanding.

What happened? The lesson I learned was that ultimately the healing needed was mine not hers! I have logged many miles on this quest. I have visited my mother's birthplace, have gone back several times to my birthplace and spent quality time with my mother at her home in Las Vegas.

I can admit to myself and the universe the role I played in creating the disconnect with my mother. This has not always been easy to do. But I swore to myself that I would be totally honest with me about all the emotions I was experiencing. So up came the Truth and I no longer hid from it. I needed to look at the scenario differently. Perhaps there was another side to this story.

My step father departed this physical world in 1993. My mother and Odis, my step father had relocated and returned to Louisiana to live many years before. But Odis wanted to be buried in Los Angeles where his oldest brother would be able to visit with him if he chose to.

A trip back to Louisiana had to be made to handle legal and other matters. I was the one to accompany my mother on this journey. It was during this trip that I did not honor my mother; for whatever reason(s) I refused to hear her pain. I did not acknowledge the void in her life. It was not done maliciously rather it was subtle. Little attention was given to assisting her with healing or coping with her pains.

I know we both are strong willed and that might have been what happened. We needed each other. We were both mourning. Perhaps each thinking their pain was greater than the other. Not understanding both were equally deserving of expressing their grief. And because I didn't, wouldn't or couldn't be that which she longed most for, she withdrew from me. Her pain was real and deep.

Maybe I just couldn't handle it. Perhaps I was still attempting to resolve issues from my childhood. Honestly right now I just do not know. The pain escalated and the separation was actualized. The blow up was the result of my not respecting her grief. The distance grew between us as we drove side by side from Los Angeles to Louisiana.

They say 'hind sight is always 20/20.' Now I fully understand the meaning in that phrase. I accept responsibility for my contributions to this situation. I could still choose to hide my hands as if I had no part in this, you know play the victim mentality game. We must look deep in our own hearts for Truth. Our words and actions have a way of playing like a ricochet, always coming back to us.

How have you created the scenarios in your life that causes you not to be able to rest comfortably? What role did you play in this confusion? Be honest with yourself even if you choose to not disclose it to anyone else. There are no victims, only willing volunteers. We forget its our thoughts that create and manifest our reality. Could it be that which you want from someone is exactly what you refuse to give to them?

Preparing for a trip to Las Vegas I sent an email to my nephew, A.K.. I told A.K. that healing was to take place when I arrived. I invited A.K. to be present if he chose to participate. I explained I was not sure who would be involved; I just knew that healing would happen.

On our drive from the airport, A.K. asked a very profound question. He asked me, "So <u>who</u> is going to be healed?" As I sat in the passenger seat of his convertible Corvette with the top down, enjoying the wonderful scenery of the mountains I contemplated my response. A.K. and I are closely connected spiritually and he serves as a mirror to my soul. I finally answered, "I don't know." A.K. smiled that huge smile of his and with powerful words of wisdom he said, "Good, because Big Mama don't need healing. She is perfectly fine the way she is." Big Mama is the name affectionately used by my mother's grandchildren.

I knew A.K. was perfectly correct. God had arranged for me to purchase, take on the airplane and read Don Miguel Ruiz's master piece 'The Voice of Knowledge'. I had heard of the author's most popular work, 'The Four Agreements' but not this book. While in a store waiting for pictures to be developed, I wandered to the book section of the store. The store carried three of Don Miguel's books and I purchased all three. I said to myself I would read them one day. I had no immediate plans to read them.

Anyway, what happened was I carried two of the books on the plane with me. I now understand I was directed to read 'The Voice of Knowledge' prior to arriving in Las Vegas. This book is so poignant and very timely. This is what I read, on my way to a healing session at my mother's house.

"I used to believe I knew my mother, but the only thing I knew about her is the role I assign her to play in my story" WOW. *"I have an image for the character who plays the role of my mother. Everything I know about her is what I believe about her."* Reading this made me twitch in my seat. I felt as if my world had stopped or at least it was now going in slow motion. As I continued to read I knew that was surely God working and leading me.

"Your mother...has no idea what you have in your mind. She only knows what she believes about you, which means she knows almost nothing. Your mother creates an image of you and she wants you to fit the image she creates." This is certainly words of knowledge and a sincere awakening for me.

So I answered A.K. saying, "The healing is for me!"

I arrived at my mother's house with no expectations, no hidden agendas, no preconceived thoughts of how everything needed to look. I just wanted to listen to her, to truly hear her. I had no control issues, no need to be right. My mother had already told me she has earned the right to sleep in late and that is how she now lives. So I knew not to wake her if I woke up early.

I awoke the next morning at 4am, I was still on East coast time. I was very quiet because I did not want to disturb my mother's sleep. I rumbled through the kitchen cabinets until I found all the necessary ingredients for my morning ritual. I found the coffee pot, the coffee, the filters, sugar and creamer. After preparing my cup of coffee I went outside to sit on the patio.

It was about 4:30am and very peaceful. No movement by anyone, no sounds of cars or other vehicles, no human expressions. The wind was gently blowing. Everything was Perfect! My mother has two wind chimes hanging in her perfect patio. God gently blew the winds to create a most beautiful melody with the chimes. I retrieved my tape recorder from the house and recorded these wonderful sounds for over two hours. One chime, then another, sometimes they both were playing their beautiful music at the same time.

During this perfect meditation time I was reminded of God's unconditional love, the love that would and could soothe my soul! Holy Spirit carefully rocked me into a complete state of thanksgiving.

I thought on the awesome love of my beautiful mother; a woman who did a great job of birthing and raising six very different and unique children.

A mother who gave her best to each of us. A mother who loved us unconditionally. A mother who only wanted the best for her children.

In that moment, in that silence – God smiled on me and healed my heart! In that moment I became abundantly joyous and elated. I was filled with compassion.

So I know the value in being connected to Source. The Creator desires we each live in honor, humility, integrity, absolute understanding, wisdom and pure, unconditional love.

When God Leads…..just follow!

Sandy Rodgers

Chapter Seven

AND THEN THERE WAS *ONE*

The last several years my work and attention has been involved with discussion and program development dealing with the affects of HIV/AIDS.

About twenty years ago I was personally affected by someone living with a full blown case of AIDS. This person was a good friend of my younger brother, Rudy Odis Brown. Rudy was killed in 1980 by a man who hit him as he crossed the street less than a block from his home. The driver of the car that killed two people, my brother and the passenger in the car, was high on drugs, PCP among other drugs. Somehow, surely by God's grace and mercy, our family was able to totally forgive this man. Not to suggest it was easy, just that it was done.

Rudy and Dennis were close friends. Dennis eventually became a welcomed addition of our extended family.

After suffering the trauma of Rudy's death, it became increasingly difficult for my mother and step father, Rudy's dad to continue living in their house. They had buried one of their children and I am sure that is a lost that can be devastating to a parent. My mother said she would see Rudy in the house and hear him speaking.

Odis just could not bear the loss. And they decided to sell the house and move away from Los Angeles. This large spacious home had a five unit apartment building in the rear. This had been home for a long time but the time had come to move out from the now ever present sadness that it represented.

Dennis purchased the property. Dennis and his mom were now the proud owners of this property. They loved the big house with three levels. They gave elaborate parties. Dennis often displayed his creative and artistic expression.

One day I was asked had I seen Dennis lately. I was told he had been sick. The person did not or would not tell me the cause of his sickness. I made several attempts to contact him by phone all with no success. I did not stop until I reached him. So eventually I contacted Dennis. I was so happy to finally talk with him. I knew Rudy would have visited him and known of his illness. I felt compelled to visit, this would honor my brother. I told Dennis I was coming to visit with him. His voice was hesitant but he agreed I could stop by for a visit.

Upon my arrival, his mother answered the door. She had a very peculiar look in her eyes. A kind of, 'I'm afraid,' look to her. I greeted her and told her I was there to see and visit with Dennis. She said she would go and get him for me.

As Dennis' frail body descended the massive stairway I saw and felt his pain. It appeared he was experiencing excruciating pain to come down those stairs.

When he noticed the concerned look on my face he told me not to worry it would be okay. He just needed to take his time in moving about and it would take him a while to make it all the way to the bottom of the stairs. I had no idea of what to expect when I finally would see him.

I embraced Dennis with all of the love I had for him. I was hugging him not only for myself but also for my deceased brother, Rudy. It was funny because he said my grip on him actually hurt. I was hugging him too tightly! I apologized but Dennis said it was okay because he had not felt that kind of love and affection in a long time.

I asked why he hadn't told me. His reply was very emotional, longing for understanding. He explained most people, his friends, did not want to be around him. They were afraid of contracting his disease, once they discovered he had AIDS. No one would dare touch him! That was awfully upsetting to me. I said it made no difference to me why he was sick or what he had, I Loved HIM anyway!

There I was embracing him as he shed tears of acceptance from me, tears of joy and love. Dennis was extremely weak. He made his way to the couch where he laid down. I sat there cradling him in my arms, just plain loving him with all that I had.

We talked for hours. We shared until he was exhausted and required rest. I left hugging him again and telling him how much I loved him. I departed knowing that I had made a difference in this man's life, a life that he shared so freely with those he loved. It was difficult for me to understand how folks could abandon him especially now in his hour of need.

My next personal encounter with this pandemic of AIDS was twenty years later on my trip to Ghana West Africa. I met some of the leaders of African Heritage

Youth Club. We communicated frequently after my return to Atlanta.

I was asked and gratefully accepted the prestigious position of Mother of this organization. I was honored to be considered to serve in this capacity. I never undertake a position without full responsibility and accountability for my contribution to the overall success of it.

So from accepting this position I asked what I could do for the organization. The African Heritage Youth Club was very active in educating the population on HIV/AIDS; sexual abstinence and how the disease is contracted. They were extremely professional in all of their activities.

They provided written documentation of the research they had completed. They went into the countryside where people were not exposed to information nor received materials that could educate them on this disease. There would be long periods of time where they did not nor could not communicate with me because they were in an area that did not have internet or cell phone access.

Sometimes, they would call me here in Atlanta. The entire club would be present. They would all join together in shouting out their love to me. Or they would sing a song. I felt goose bumps as I listened closely to their expressions of love and gratitude. It is always an incredible event to receive a call, a package or mail from the Club.

Later that same year I learned of a grant that targeted Ghana and children affected by HIV/AIDS. The grant would fund programs whose work dealt with the Psycho-Social Affects of HIV/AIDS on Children.

When I finally told my brother William what I was working on, he became excited and offered to help with program development. Once word got out about the project Keep America Strong was creating, gathering a team of dedicated individuals whose hearts were entwined with those suffering in Africa was easy. The project is called; **Total Wellness Project - Education, Health and Economics.**

For six months the team of ten to fifteen, conducted weekly conference calls to develop a holistic approach to this pandemic. Experts from every field that required addressing generously participated and shared their knowledge with the group.

The program encompasses health, education and economics. The group researched and presented their findings weekly on the conference calls. The group consisted of experts from around the nation that possessed knowledge and proven treatments for the cure and eradication of the disease.

Our team members include an Epidemiologist, Naturopath Doctor, Education Specialist, Community Organizers, Business Professionals, Clinician, Youth Advocates, AIDS Specialists, Health Professionals, Clothing Textile representatives, Construction/Builders, Art Education Therapist, Finance/Accountant, Program Developers and Local Ghanaian Organizers.

The final program is being considered by groups in South Africa and Ghana. We are awaiting funding for this worthy program which includes all the components described by the African Heritage Youth Club as being vital to the overall health of Africa. As we await the funding sources, we continue with our respective work. All are very eager to serve others to offer their expertise in the healing of this pandemic that is affecting the entire universe.

In April of 2006, I was asked by the Program Director, Rev. James Suber, if I would come and be a guest speaker for the group at Atlanta InterFaith AIDS

Network. I was extremely happy to participate, to talk with the group. Well, **When God Leads,** you never know exactly where you are going or why you doing what you are doing. Trusting the process though will definitely lead you into miraculous adventures.

As I shared my personal story with the group, some did not believe I was telling them the truth. They felt this way because of the vividness of my past. Some felt I was making it all up just to be accepted.

However as I shared they all learned I could not tell the story the way I did unless I had personal experience in the areas I addressed. Some were shocked at my revelations to them of the many ugly situations that I had encountered in life.

Some wanted to know why I would tell about my past, especially with my present title of Reverend. The point was to get the group to understand that we all have a story. Some may say they have not had any challenges but most do! So I share mine freely, it helps others to open up and tell their story. I tell them about drug use and abuse, abandonment issues, not loving myself, alcoholism and mere existing.

The first engagement was so incredible that I agreed to come back and speak again to the group. We went beyond the allotted one hour time by several minutes actually about fifteen minutes. And this became natural and normal for us. I then spoke with them more often. First once a month, then twice a month, to weekly to finally being involved on a daily basis; I am now called the Resident Therapist, with love of course.

These individuals are truly my extended family. I love each one sincerely. We have built a wonderful trust system that beckons each person to dig deep to uncover the hidden lies they have accepted as their truth. The deceptions have mostly first appeared in their childhood. It has been very painful for some to remember their trauma. For others it has been extremely difficult to forgive the person or persons they feel responsible for inflicting the pain they now feel.

But we, as a family, have worked through each person's grief. Within a loving atmosphere each has shared themselves to the group. Often this is done with tears, which is encouraged. They must feel the pain and not mask it or call it something that it is not. I dare them to just try what I am suggesting. I never tell them they are wrong for what they feel.

I allow them to label themselves in whatever way they choose. But I do suggest a different approach: An approach of regarding themselves as worthy, lovable children of the Most High God, Creator.

I tell them in no uncertain terms that they are good regardless to what is showing up in their lives now. They are not cursed or will go to hell for the sins they have committed. I ask and gently persuade them to look at things at a slightly different angle.

I speak there weekly with joy and appreciation. This is my family. I give them my best because they deserve the best. I love them individually and collectively unconditionally.

Some have never been shown or given unconditional love before. They are at first uncomfortable in receiving it and allowing it to touch them. But these are some wonderful individuals seeking truth and desiring better for themselves and their families. They are incredible folks beating the odds against them. They are strong and loving people.

Some have experienced illnesses or hospitalization since I have been participating with the group. We have grown so much in love and acceptance, of forgiveness and release. The stories shared are real for the person, so it makes no difference if anyone else believes or accepts them as real or not. When we can each share our story without judgments or criticism we can begin to heal that wounded-ness in our soul.

Some have fought hard not to cooperate and have believed the lies and the labels given to them by society. I just laugh at them and ask them to try it anyway. When they do and it works they gladly share what miracles happened in their lives as a direct result of doing what I asked them to do. I smile with joy when they tell the group they have finally been able to forgive and release the past.

I am overjoyed when they tell me they have contacted a parent after many years of total separation. And when someone finally shares their story after being an inactive part of the group for six months it literally brings tears to my heart, soul and eyes. I embrace their growth and surrender with unconditional love and support.

For those who have accepted and believed they had to call themselves junkies, addicts or recovering, I asked them one day to change their thought.

What if they were actually cured and the only thing standing in the way was their acceptance and acknowledgement of this fact? Boy oh boy did I hear a vast variety of solidly held reasons why they could not do that. "If I forget where I came from I might go back there." So my question was why not go back to a place of innocence, a place in time before you became that which you do not want to be any longer. Go back to the time before the abuse started within the family. Go back to the place where you were a child, a time of perfection.

These individuals are healing every single day! They are shining brightly their lights of life! They simply glow with a radiance of joy!

The healing has been two way, for them and me. As I pushed and challenged them, I pushed myself. We each had to remember, forgive, release and replace those situations with love. It may never end because sometimes we bury a lot of junk in our memory bank.

We hide it so that we do not have to deal with it again. We think that if we can't recall it, it will go away. But as we have learned it does not go away it just goes deeper into us. It gets to a level in our consciousness that eventually makes us sick. We suffer from all sorts of ailments and disease not necessarily because of anything other than it has been eating away at us for so long it starts to attack our systems because we will not nor do not know how to release it.

My unorthodox methods generally catch people by surprise. People are surprised because of the love I give without any regard to receiving it back in return.

I shine my light for everyone to see and feel. It does not matter what your story is, we are all connected to the same Source of Life, The Creator of all things created both you and me. We are each in this big gigantic unit called a family. So it does not matter if you live in Australia, Asia, or the United States. For that matter it does not make a difference if you reside in Ohio, Iowa or South Dakota, we still are family.

When we interact with others as family, a healthy family, we connect differently. We connect with love, encouragement, peace, joy, harmony, support and sincerity.

My most rewarding work has been with people affected with HIV/AIDS. Not because I am clinically educated but rather that I have passion and compassion for all humanity.

Deep inside the crevices of their souls they feel tremendous pain. Not necessarily due to the illness rather it's due to all the negative stigmas that are placed on them.

Remember my friend Dennis? He was willing to die without the love and support of any of his friends.

My message is: "You are a child of GOD".

My Beloved Family, You and I are one. There is no difference between us. We are from the same Source. We are One Family. We are One Life. We are One Energy!!!

When God Leads…just follow!

Where is God leading you that you refuse to go? Do not be fearful of the journey. Why are you not fulfilling that deep passion in your heart????

When God Leads…just follow!

Chapter Eight

HEALING THOUGHTS

My work is helping people, including myself to heal. This has been my mission in life since 1990 or earlier. I clearly remember writing it down in 1990 on paper. God always speaks to me. There have been times in my life when I did not recognize 'the voice'. Some time it was due to the fact I had numbed myself with drugs, alcohol or sex. Anything worked.

Anything, that is, that could prevent me from hearing the well intentioned voices that yelled at me, 'You are no good!' The internal chatter that kept me looking 'out there', outside of me, for my hope and salvation. The thousand tongues and languages that insisted I would never, ever be enough.

Yet even during the most distressed times, my spiritual self kept me from complete despair. Suicidal thoughts as a teenager had me to keep a razor blade under my pillow.

Drugs, drugs and more drugs were my constant companion. Weed, acid, cocaine, pills, alcohol, but the greatest danger I suffered had nothing to do with what I was ingesting. It was the untruths that I believed about myself that placed the authentic me in a comatose state for many, many years.

Even in the midst of my self imposed prison of hell, God kept leading me; leading me away from death, and leading me towards a brighter today and future.

I felt I could never give up. I may slip. I may fall. I may even take other people down with me yet I could not stay there, down. I may have been down but never completely out; out of life, out of God's grace and mercy.

During my twenties I recognized I was clairvoyant. I would and could have visions and dreams about situations before they actually occurred. And then when they were manifested physically, it frightened me.

I knew not to confess this gift to anyone. I thought people would think I was crazy or merely exaggerating – you know they would think I was lying! With all the other demons dancing in my mind I dare not open up additional discussion about my sanity.

So I would not develop or use my gift. I allowed it to die by not feeding it; withholding oxygen from it. My gift died a premature death due to fear of being more than I was led to believe I could be. 'Children should be seen and not heard' was a familiar restrictive phrase I heard. 'Women are only worthy if they have a husband' was another one of my favorite limiting concepts. 'Men don't want intelligent women because that strength in a woman intimidates a man'.

I was already ashamed of who I was; high yellow (bright complexion), plump, unattractive and simply a physical object or toy for men (At least those were my identifying traits given to me by others). Recently I admitted to my two best girlfriends, Criss and Candace, that breaking up with a boyfriend I had dated for several years during my senior high school days had devastated me.

As I said the words out loud, I told them as I wondered to myself where is this coming from? Surely it was not from cool, always in control of herself Sandy saying this. We all enjoyed a good laugh about my total disclosure, my shedding the mask for truth!

All I could feel in my heart was healing. I am dedicated to healing, telling my truth of the past, feeling all the emotions attached, releasing, forgiving, and loving each incident. This is what I do! This is my work. So I tell my story in as much honesty as the listener can bear.

I have learned to look at and witness the pain associated with those situations and speak healing to them. Just because that boyfriend found another girlfriend never really defined my worthiness. My denial and refusal to release him was actually my garbage.

That part of my story reinforced the lies I had been told about me. Lies I had thought were my truth of being. I was a young innocent lady who truly believed that losing this guy made me unlovable, unattractive and completely unworthy. Wow, all these years, almost forty! And I am just recognizing where I learned how to be dependent on someone for my definition and value.

But really, what do any of these things have to do with me and who I am? The ultimate answer is absolutely nothing. I am not those things, I am not those thoughts.

So who gets the grand opportunity to define me now? After fifty years of allowing and accepting others opinion of me I have finally determined and I am steadfastly convinced – I am the only one who can define me!

Anything other than what I declare I am is just someone's opinion. And I also know without any doubt, that every living human has an opinion. And! I have the right, by my divinity, to not accept anything from anyone because it is merely their perception. Perception is neither real or false; good or bad; perception is as individual as finger prints.

So I listen and respect each person's story, their perception of reality. No one can rightly judge, criticize, condemn, or condone it. This simple act of kindness adds value to the person I communicate with. What I think, is truly none of their business. To be heard is the greatest gift we can give to another. Just listen. The process of listening is so profound, so healing for the teller of the story.

The key is to listen without judgment. Know your only requirement is to listen. Do not offer advice. Do not correct the story. The story, as it is being told, is absolutely true for that person! Who really cares if you agree or not?

The art of listening offers wondrous rewards. You, as the listener, develop an acceptance that is without conditions. Your heart is enriched. You become one with the story-teller. No competition. No comparisons. When the teller of the story requires no justification, they feel valued. The inner spirit is honored and respected.

And if your story is of pain, the pain you experience is yours! No one will ever be able to feel your injustice, if any exist for you. But you keep telling the story. In hopes of somehow conveying the incident in such a way that maybe one day another person will know just how bad it was for us. We never pause long enough to know that that is impossible. Your story is Your Story! Your pain is Your Pain. Your perception is your reality!

Isn't it amazingly incredible that you possess something no one living or dead can possess? That one thing is YOU and your story! So please excuse me if I can't feel your pain. And forgive me if I do not react the way you need or want me.

I can guarantee that I will be fully present in the moment with you, as I truly listen. I promise to hear you without judgment. I will listen with the ears of love. I will embrace your every thought.

When you allow and follow God's guidance you end up in very interesting places and situations. You must just be in the present moment. The present moment is always a gift.

In the receiving of the gift there is no worry about the past or any fear of the future. You truly enjoy your precious gift, which is the ultimate unfolding of life. Unplanned and unscheduled. Simply sitting in the splendor of Now!

In this present moment you may find yourself surrounded by those you love and who loves you. In this present moment you have a choice. You can choose to release any and all past actions. You may choose to soak in the beauty of what is. What is, right now.

Do you secretly desire Love, Peace and/or Happiness? Know that in this present moment it is yours! No action is required of you. That's right no physical exertion. It is simply a choice, your choice; a mental conscious decision to be exactly that which you desire.

In this present moment you may or may not like the outer workings, the physical manifestations of your previous choices. You can change the circumstances by changing your thought.

That feeling is an inner urging to suggest to you a change is needed. If you could wave a magic wand and make a change, what would you change? You possess the magic wand. The magic wand is your thought.

Your prominent thoughts are always revealed as your life. Believe it or not thought is powerful and vibrant. Your life reflects your thoughts. Don't like what you see? Think A New Thought.

I had a wonderful experience with one of my best friends, who also happen to be my ex-husband. Our story is so long. It's fascinating, wild and incredible. Initially we built a strong relationship on friendship and we were the best of friends.

However a few years and several dares (that's correct dares not dates!) later we found ourselves living together as husband and wife. In that place of marriage we lost our foundation, our friendship.

In completing the cycle, we are currently back at our starting point of sharing a fabulous friendship. I can and am so openly honest with my thoughts and feelings. I have someone who listens without feeling a need to solve my challenges, who allows me to just be me.

We had dinner then took a long leisurely walk along the ocean. Later we strolled down the main street, Ocean Boulevard. When we had lived together in this community years earlier it had not been revitalized; thirteen years later it was full of new energy, new life, just like our relationship. This area was symbolic of part of our life together.

Sidewalk cafes and bistros lined the street. Colorful, happy and friendly people of all ages greeted each other as they passed. In the middle of the street, which was barricaded, there was an antique car display, a clown, a ballerina and at the far end of the street a live band performing. People were dancing in the street and truly enjoying life.

We got coffee and sat outside at a small table. We continued to talk and share. The scenery was all new to me. But I thoroughly appreciated the beauty of our renewed friendship. He got it too!

Maybe our marriage was just a training for him. He says he learned a lot from me that he now applies in his current relationship. Most times when I compliment him on his actions, his response is, "Well I learned that from you."

It's funny. I was looking for validation in our marriage. Yet in our friendship I already had personal validation. After all these years I can finally admit that I felt resentful that what I thought I needed and could only get in a marriage I already possessed. And it was not my husband or anyone else's responsibility to give that to me.

I am still growing; still in the process of unlearning false concepts; still releasing outside influences and dependencies. I am choosing only wholeness and total self responsibility.

Sandy Rodgers

Chapter Nine

MY JOURNEY TO MINISTRY

There I was in the perfect job, the job of my dreams and I was very content. My position was Director of Programs, Public Relations and Continuing Spiritual Education. My place of employment was Hillside Chapel and Truth Center, Rev. Dr. Barbara King, Founder/Minister.

I enjoyed the daily challenges my position offered. I loved working with the members. As Program Director I had the awesome opportunity of helping individuals and groups coordinate and conduct various activities. With an extensive background in program development I was amply prepared to assist those wanting to present their program proposal. It was all done very professionally with business plans, course outlines or whatever was required. The individuals involved appreciated the professional approach and environment.

In the Public Relations Department I represented Hillside in the community. Attending meetings and networking always yielded perfect opportunities to expand Hillside's presence in the community. We hosted a wide variety of projects. We took the lead in several community based events. Creating collaborations within the community of businesses and other religious groups.

The Continuing Spiritual Education Department was an excellent venue to provide quality classes and instructors to the membership. The creation of an educational pamphlet was a great addition to the existing department.

In addition to these duties, Hillside was my family. I made numerous friendships that were dear to my heart. The elders became my Dads and Moms.

Always welcoming visitors to the church was a small but very important aspect of my responsibilities. I spent a great deal of time entertaining visitors and guests to Hillside. Regardless to the occasion, be it a special guest on Sunday or another day of the week. I appreciated increasing my knowledge of people. I enjoyed meeting, sharing with and serving the many that came to our place of worship, our home.

I was sought after, approached to lead a rather newly created company as its General Manager. I remained open to the possibility of learning and growing in a new industry. So after many months of being courted and negotiating with the owner I finally agreed to accept the position.

I was fascinated with learning all the intricacies of creating and promoting various recording artists. I was responsible for the design of the website and its content. I wrote all the articles that appeared on the site. I met regularly with the technical team who were the site administrators to ensure we had a quality product.

The visits to the studio to work with the recording artists were exciting. Developing their image and selecting the photos for the album covers was stimulating. I loved this new career!

Pastor Carl Booker is a friend of mine. I had met and worked with Pastor Booker several years earlier with Preach and Teach Ministries. His main focus was doing street ministry. They would go into the shelters and hold prayer services in the neighborhood. In getting to know

Pastor Booker, I discovered he was a very talented singer and composer.

When I was searching for new artists for the label company I contacted Pastor Booker to arrange for a meeting. During the meeting I explained the direction of the music company, the positive and powerful influence the impact of the music would have on the world. Pastor Booker shared his music with me during my visit.

Once that part of our meeting was completed, Pastor Booker said he wanted to discuss another matter with me. Always loving his spirit and the work he does, I eagerly agreed.

Pastor Booker advised me he was reorganizing his church and he was extremely proud and pleased to report it to me. And as he continued he actually paused, took a long penetrating look into my eyes and said, "Sister Sandy I have always been impressed by your compassion for people. The women you worked with at the shelter still ask about you. So I know you made a difference in their lives." He paused again. Then he said, "I want you to consider heading the Women's Ministry of Preach and Teach Ministries." I was filled with humility and was speechless. I just sat there. I thanked Pastor Booker for this awesome opportunity. I told him I would pray and meditate then advise him when I reached a decision.

WOW! I said to myself as I got into my car. 'Okay God what are we doing now?' Pastor Booker had said he would ordain me when I completed all the necessary class work and required papers.

I had to get away. What a powerful and humbling offering. I refused to rush a decision. I had to be certain. My prayer was for clarity. I was told to go to the mountain top by 'the voice'.

The following two pieces were written in my solitude while away contemplating an answer to Pastor Booker's proposal.

Room 104

Two days before leaving for my much anticipated get away my sister angel - Pamelaia Sanders advised me of my three core numbers which are 1, 4 and 5.

My original plan was to leave Saturday morning. On Friday afternoon God whispered to me, 'Why are you waiting? You are ready to go.' I had rushed around all day to be fully prepared to leave the next morning. It was 4pm, the beginning of rush hour traffic on a Friday afternoon in Atlanta. I thought to myself I'll wait until 6pm. Spirit then spoke louder 'Leave Now!' So I packed quickly. I had this rushed energy to get going. By 5pm my car was packed with all the items from my previously prepared list. It definitely was God moving me because Sandy had told herself that she could stay home and just let people think she was gone. The movement was truly not mine. By 5:15pm I was pulling out of my driveway. I was only two blocks away when I realized I had forgotten half of my money. I turned around and resolved that issue.

Traffic was indeed heavy and I decided to stop and eat dinner. I remembered I had not eaten all day. I had been too consumed in working and preparing for the trip.

I stopped and had dinner. I had left my cell phone in the car. My son Malcolm called very excited, telling me to have a great time. Said he knew I would be turning off my cell phone. He just laughed when I confirmed he was absolutely correct. As soon as I reached my destination the phone would be turned off!

The interstate was still crowded and it was 7pm. I thought it would have thinned out by now. But not a problem, its moving regardless to how fast or slow as the case was. The drive was relaxing. No noise in my car, just me.

    In a short time I had arrived at my destination of Chattanooga Tennessee. Spirit chose this place for me, said go to the mountains. And within hours on that day Malcolm was showing me some special room rates in Chattanooga. I thought about making reservations, being the organized person that I am. I had picked up my mail from the Post Office which contained my credit card statement and my balance left me with a mere $15.00 available credit. "Let's go," said Spirit.

    I first stopped at Marriott where the room rate was $126.00. The man behind the counter said he could give me a discount if I had an AAA card which I did. He said "Okay the rate will be $123.00", I laughed and said No thanks. I will look somewhere else. The lady beside him commented on my Christmas attire. What was the reason I left was not about the price. I discovered this as I drove away. This hotel was within a short walking distance from the mall. I knew I had come to meditate and being able to walk to stores would certainly cause me anxiety. So I laughed and drove off. On the other side of the interstate were a row of Hotel chains that I recognized. At the end of the cul de sac was Country Inns and Suites. That's where I will stay. I pulled up and parked my car. Went inside to inquire about availability, the pleasant lady advised me they had rooms. I checked in, received my room card and went back outside to move my car and get my belongings. As I was walking out I looked at my room card and my room was – 104! The desk clerk had offered me a change of rooms, one with double beds and the other with a king bed which was a handicap room facility. She explained the only difference with the handicap room was everything was lower and the bathroom had hand rails. So I opted for the king bed handicap room.

It took me several trips to get everything out of the car. I brought 2 CD players, food, candles, and my clothes. I unpacked and settled in.

I decided to begin my meditation weekend on Friday night. So I relaxed on the comfy couch and listened to two tapes from my Holosync series, *Making Change Easy* and *Super Longevity*. I was in a zone, a wonderfully powerful zone. I had very important matters to decide this weekend. I was in a marvelous place of absolute Peace as I wrote out my feelings and revelations. Clarity, Understanding, and Wisdom all came to stay with me. It was refreshing and welcomed. My Spirit is soaring because I have discovered, allowed myself to be completely open and receptive to the Truth.

Off to sleep. I attempted to watch TV but I couldn't. Back to the meditation tapes. I drifted off listening to 'Super Longevity'.

Woke refreshed and feeling great. Got dressed to go get some coffee and fruit from the Hotel's breakfast area. Shared some words of encouragement and compassion to the hotel workers whose responsibility was to stock the breakfast foods. Some folks can be very wonderful while being rude and disrespectful. Anyway I got her to smile and not give any attention to the negative situation. As I walked back to my room I realized it was 104! How significant that Pamelaia just advised me of my power/destiny numbers of 1, 4 and 5.

I am excited about receiving full advantage of being in this my room of destiny. And the rate is $104.00! Wow God how awesome is this? Okay Sandy get yourself Ready – Blessings – Release – Renewal!

I had only paid for one night when I checked in. I didn't know then the significance of this room. So I am off to extend my stay for another night. Actually had planned on staying, so I cannot really say why I only paid for one night upon checking in. Part of it was accepting I am worthy and deserving of staying in a nice establishment like this by myself. And I am so into it, really enjoying myself.

I played my music. I listened to Rickie Byars Beckwith. As I listen I am placed in a very sentimental and spiritual mood. In her song Pray For Me, I pushed the repeat button because the melody and words touched me very deeply. "There's a blessing in every breath" How awesome God is!

Tears well up in my eyes as I remember how wonderfully blessed I am. God is simply pouring out one miracle after another upon me. Someone is praying for me. Thanks God for ALL MY ANGELS. Too numerous to count them all but they are all around the globe. Some close and some far away. Yet each is holding me up in love and prayer. Some are even on the other side of this physical life.

So here I sit, overwhelmingly filled with Gratitude and Love! I have made a conscious decision to stay inside Room 104 the entire day. Perhaps tomorrow I'll go to Lookout Mountain. I celebrate me! I celebrate my unique femininity, my beauty, my Spirit.

As I relax into this peace I am listening to "My Destiny Has Been fulfilled by God. I Rest in Thee! My search is over. Every path had led me to this moment. Something in me knew this all along my life is a melody of God's freedom song. I rest in Thee. My destiny has been fulfilled by You, oh God. I rest in Thee." Thanks Rickie.

And the second writing:

My Ancestors Are Having A Party!

My Ancestors are throwing a big bash. They are celebrating my life! I am the guest of Honor and proud to stand in that special place.

They are all, each one, welcoming you to be a guest; to join them in a glorious party of Dancing, fellowshipping, laughter and JOY.

They are telling me I have done a good job with my life. Each has guided me, gently as I veered off course. They understood however that I needed to travel down that particular path to reach my destiny. But I know some of those crooks in the road that I ventured down had them squenching with concern. They held me in their LOVE. That is always a cherished space for me. They caress me, wipe my tears and assure me, 'It's All Good!'

So I prepare myself to be honored. I do what I do in Love and Truth. I keep reaching, stretching beyond my comfort levels. I have had to learn lessons to receive the Blessings. And yes, some lessons I repeated the experiences until I really 'got it'.

My Ancestors are cheering me on to higher levels, to higher Christ consciousness. They are urging, sometimes pushing me to keep going. I am so thankful. So filled with appreciation and gratitude. They are chanting, in unison, 'Go Sandy Go!' I hear them and I keep going and going. I do not even think about back sliding or stopping.

That weekend served to remind me of some earlier experiences that assisted me on my oath towards spiritual enlightenment and awakening.

During a Dolphin Meditation I saw them very clearly, standing on the shoreline as I emerged from my under water journey. Jumping up and down, grinning with full excitement and encouragement. I began to weep with

Joy! For at that very moment I fully accepted the Love and Support of my Ancestors. I completely realized how what I am doing with my life is pleasing to them. I am humbled by my receptivity to their Wisdom. I stand tall in their LOVE, STRENGTH, POWER, COURAGE AND PASSION.

About a year or so earlier, events unfolded to reveal a process which now serves me in making my decision about the ministry. I was in the sacred presence of Dr. Mark Armstrong, Ahimki Center for Wholeness. I had the pleasure of meeting Dr. Mark as he was one of the presenters at a Fibroid Tumor Conference. I was impressed with his medical/holistic knowledge, verbal presentation, his sensitivity to the health care field, his sincere spirituality and his genuine compassion for women. And when he said he was from Compton California, I knew I had to meet him. I could not rest until I got an opportunity to talk with him. I had gone to the conference as a vendor and a co-sponsor, meeting Dr. Mark was a bonus, a blessing.

Hillside was hosting its second Health Fair and I highly recommended Dr. Mark be included and he was. On the day of the Health Fair, Dr. Clinton Carter was introducing me to the presenters that I did not know. When he got to Dr. Mark he said, "Well I know you know Sandy. She is the reason you are here today. She speaks so highly of you." Dr. Mark thanked me. I had actually forgotten my insistence on having him included. Dr. Mark's presentation included statements about what people 'think' is in their DNA. He expressed concern that our DNA includes not only genetic gene sharing but family thoughts and eating habits passed down from one generation to the next. His words touched me deeply. This was another messenger with the same message that we *pass along unhealthy and unresolved issues from one branch of the family tree to the next.*

I could not rest until I got an opportunity to talk with him. I told Dr. Mark about my latest book, 'The Rose Garden' and my strong belief that people especially women must tell their story to free themselves and acknowledge their worthiness. I felt it was not until that cleansing moment that an individual can open up, honor themselves and become receptive to hearing powerful positive messages. My belief is that in honoring our story exactly as we remember it, we allow ourselves to feel more love and accept our own worthiness.

Dr. Mark was impressed with my passion and asked me to make an appointment at his office so that we could continue our conversation. Dr. Mark said, "Many are hurting and desire healing. I can't do it alone. I welcome people like you to help me in this work."

It took me awhile before I finally called and made the appointment. Dr. Mark began the appointment with a healing session. I believe this practice assisted him in being more spiritually connected to me. During our conversation and sharing Dr. Mark gleamed and told me, "Your Ancestors are very pleased with you. They are happy to see you do the work they started; to give names and recognition to the many nameless children, and to do your work in this healing process." I was so humbled and I knew my ancestors had revealed their knowledge of me to Dr. Mark. I left his office floating spiritually. I knew I had powerful work to do. I accept the Calling. I believe this meeting took place in June.

And then, many months later, on December 15th, my seer, my connection to my Ancestors, Timothy Branch had a message for me. Tim told me my Ancestors were pleased with me. He said they are celebrating in the traditional manner; with the drums and its powerful beats, chanting praises and dancing! I told Tim I felt it. Tim is a very dear friend of mine. And the cousin of a man I call my soul mate. Whenever I visit the two of them I am greeted with huge amounts of love and acceptance. Tim has been revealing to me the visions and messages that he receives from the other side. He is highly gifted in his connection with Spirit, the ancestors and seeing into the future. I believe in the work Tim does. I welcome his sharing with me. Tim is an open vessel and receptive to receiving the many messages given to him. He does not impose his messages on others. However he is very willing to share with anyone who desires the messages.

Today, December 17th, I am with my Ancestors! I am enjoying their company, their compassion and their love. We have enjoyed a wondrous time together. And its not over yet!

I am still in my preparation time for the party. Could it be they are waiting for me to make a decision? To accept the position of Minister with Preach and Teach Ministries? I feel they know I AM READY just a little reluctant in accepting my calling. SMILE! So maybe we will have this big shin- dig today, tomorrow or ? My Ancestors are loving me through this process. I feel their protection and their presence with me, Right Here, Right Now! Thanks God.

After sitting and meditating with God for two days, I was ready to return home. I had received my answer.

When I returned home I felt relaxed and refreshed. I called my childhood Pastor, Pastor C.C. Coleman. I told Pastor Coleman what had been proposed to me. And I explained my reluctance was due to the fact I had not completed course work in Theology. Pastor Coleman told me I had been ready for a long time. He knew back some twenty years earlier that I had been called into the ministry because I did the work from my heart and that is where God resides.

Pastor Coleman said "Many folks attend classes or go to seminary, yet they do not possess the gift in their heart." Then he said, "Do not be concerned with classes just keep doing the work you have always done." I was thankful to still have this wonderful Spirit with me when I needed him. Pastor Coleman continues to be my God Father, friend and Pastor.

Mother Elnor Abdullah in Fort Worth Texas was overjoyed when I explained to her what was happening in my life. She said, "Daughter, Allah has called you into a special place. I am so very proud of you! I knew all along you were a messenger."

Now I had received confirmation from two sources but still I wanted more. I made an appointment with Rev. Robert Kilgore. This man I call my Big Brother. He has always been an excellent teacher and friend. When we met I explained my concerns just as I had done with Pastor Coleman. Rev. Kilgore said he agreed with what Pastor Coleman had told me. He said I had provided healing with him on several occasions, even if I did not know at the time I was ministering to his soul and spirit. Tears were now flowing because I knew what my decision would be to Pastor Booker. I thanked my Big Brother and left.

Finally I met with Pastor Booker and advised him of my decision and acceptance of his offer. Pastor Booker beamed with delight. We discussed the schedule for the classes and preparation begun. The process was fast paced. Classes were conducted in between my already busy schedule with the music company.

After many weeks of preparation, testing and interviews by the governing board of Pastors, it was time for the Ordination ceremony.

I called Pastor Coleman the morning of the ordination. He prayed with me and told me, "Now Sandy you are in a special family. Your life will never be the same again. One thing I must tell you is that you must go wherever you are called to go."

The Ordination was very special. My closest and dearest family and friends attended. The service was incredible! Many told me after that they had attended ordination services in the past but none was as spiritual as this one. I felt it too. All my Ancestors attended, perhaps this was the Party! I know it felt like it. I saw them all there, smiling, grinning very happy and grateful that I had accepted My Calling!

My life has not been the same just as Pastor Coleman told me. I go wherever I am called to go. The healing that happens is miraculous and very welcomed. The places and people I have ministered to are as varied as one could imagine. I have gone to jails and hospitals. Visiting the sick and imprisoned. The people I serve are always left with a smile and joy. I assist them with understanding their connection to Source, to God and the Universe.

Chapter Ten

COMING FULL CIRCLE

I was born and raised in Watts, California. Watts was considered and defined as the lowest of lows in all aspects – emotionally, materially and economic conditions. The residents of this community, ghetto, were plagued with little to no self esteem and poverty was evidenced throughout.

My first home was in a little compound called Palm Lane. Although I do not know the history of its name origin, it was for families of former military men. This compound has been demolished and now Martin Luther King Jr. Hospital stands on that same piece of land. My family life began there.

During the 1960's we were blessed to live in a single family house on 115th Street. This part of 115th Street is centered between two housing projects, the Nickerson Gardens and the Imperial Courts.

Our neighborhood was very 'colorful'. Just to the east of our home was a section of town called 'The Front'. 'The Front' was a notorious part of Watts. It was home to pimps and prostitutes; wine-o's and drug addicts; it was the location of several pool halls and businesses that engaged in illicit activities such as gambling, drug trafficking and number running.

Our house was a short distance from all of this illegal activity and most days we witnessed all the wonderful events unfolding there. The pimps would stop their cars in front of or close to our house. They would literally kick their prostitutes out of their car, sometimes hitting them first yet shoving was automatically done. Perhaps the physical violence was to keep their woman in line, so that they did not forget who was in charge of them. This concept never made any logical sense to me, even as a kid.

As children would do we gave each one of them a name. Surprisingly, some of them were friendly while others could traumatize you just with their presence. We discovered that some of them were educated and had been successful in life but somehow they got reduced to mere dust-like existence. But this was where we lived. A small child being exposed to and raised in this environment could have permanent, lifelong psychological damage. The influences were too numerous to put on just a few pages. Could a child possibly dare to think outside of those limiting confines?

Today one would call our local wine-o, homeless drunks. They sat on crates and lived in cardboard boxes, in the dirt parking lot next to the liquor stores which was by the railroad tracks. There were at least three liquor stores in a quarter block area. We were always walking past them to get to wherever we were going. There were so many of them, swaying and lingering on the streets. You knew they were high on something, be it alcohol or some other drugs. They looked scary, wore dirty filthy clothes, and they smelled awful! And they hung out near our house and in our neighborhood.

The Red Car, the train system, carried passengers from Downtown Los Angeles to Long Beach. We could hear and sometimes feel the train as it passed along the tracks at Wilmington Avenue and 115th Street.

Most of our friends lived in either of the two projects. My parents always welcomed our friends and so our home became home to all. My mother always made sure there was enough food to feed every child that came to her home. My step-father proudly served as a father figure to our friends. He was forever teaching the boys about life, building, fishing and survival. We raised animals as well. We had chickens that we raised that later became our meals. We had a vegetable garden also. At one point in time we even had a Shetland pony named Tony. We were not the typical Watts family. We experienced a lot of good things along with our daily exposure to a different way of life. Having the two very contrasting ways of life certainly produced choices for us.

In the early 1960's, my brother William and I, along with a large number of our friends decided we wanted to experience something different. We were all young, pre-teens and teenagers. We were kids thinking outside the box of the stigmatism of poverty and living in Watts. We dared to think a new thought than what we were being exposed to. We formed SCFIW – Student Committee For Improvement In Watts and we went about determined to make a positive difference and change in our community. We organized ourselves, held meetings to strategize our plans and went about creating that which we desired – A community filled with folks of high self esteem and beauty.

SCFIW changed the community. We cleaned the property of the elders. We cleaned the streets. We had fun while we expanded our territory and our consciousness. We often focused on the area around Simon Rodia's Watts Towers which served as our culmination celebration location.

Our adult sponsor, Ms Sue Welsh guided and directed us to success. Ms Welsh gave very unselfishly of herself to help us achieve victory. She sought out areas that were predominately Caucasian neighborhoods for exchange opportunities. She said "Being of Irish descent, I do not accept defeat." This was the early 1960's and a white woman helping children from the ghetto was not a common sight. The racial difference was not a factor; Ms. Welsh embraced each of us as one of her children, though she was not much older than us. To this very day, Ms. Sue Welsh still encourages us to grow and make a positive impact upon the lives of everyone we encounter.

Each member of SCFIW – Student Committee For Improvement In Watts, made a pact with one another to not be like other people. We said we would all get a college education and return to contribute to Watts. We vowed not to move into the suburbs and forget about where we came from, Watts.

The Watts Riots erupted in 1964. We thought and still think today that perhaps it occurred to stop the positive work we were accomplishing. Surely we were making a positive mark on Watts and its residents. We went to City Hall to petition our local elected officials for their help. We demanded the absent business and property owners be held responsible for maintaining their property and that the city do its part in helping to keep Watts clean. The officials laughed and mocked us during our first visit. But that did not stop us! We went back and developed a more convincing argument for our politicians. We hit the streets and came back with arms full of signed petitions! We were victorious in gaining the support of the legislative body of Los Angeles. We were a force to be reckoned with, a group of determined teenagers demanding better!

No one individual or other group was giving any attention to the changing of Watts. We were the only ones bold enough to say we would not settle for the deplorable conditions we lived in. We would not settle for deteriorated vacant buildings remaining an eye sore. We said it was our responsibility to project community pride. We cleaned for our elders with no thought of compensation. It was our duty, being young and full of energy to do the work. So we did not tolerate anything less than total community improvement and upliftment.

During the Watts Riots all hell broke lose. There was fire, shootings, killings, vandalizing and people were terrified. Our house was one block over from Imperial Highway, a major street on the outskirts of Watts. We heard sirens and helicopters the entire time. Fire even graced our backyard while hot embers fell on our roof during the riots. We were right in the middle of the tragedy that overtook the community.

Fast forward some forty plus years later. My brother William and I are still doing the same kind of work. This time however we are in different parts of the country.

Yet what we have come to accept is that, although others may feel or have felt that we abandoned our initial promise to return and continue our work in Watts, the same mentality and conditions exist throughout the United States. The world has truly become a 'ghetto', with too many of our human brothers and sisters suffering from self-limiting beliefs without any real appreciation for their excellence and beauty.

We are still fulfilling our promise, just in new states.

We trust and know that it was a Force greater than us to give us that new thought to make a positive difference.

We continue with the works effecting thousands upon thousands, especially the youth, because we embrace with complete surrender to….

When God Leads….just follow.

Conclusion

I Am Thankful for my ability to communicate through the written word. I am grateful and I appreciate all the gifts that God has bestowed upon me. No, it's not always easy or convenient to welcome or use them. Yet, it is my responsibility to express Truth in whatever situation I may be in.

I give thanks for my family of origin. Each has contributed to my fullness of expression. I appreciate my extended family, those who appeared and arrived on my path to bless me.

In the final analysis, **When God Leads**…just follow, can simply be viewed as a guide for exercising a little thing called FAITH!

May God richly bless you. May you accept the Wisdom of the Inner Voice! May you discover your gifts and talents in awe!

As for me, I have completed my course work successfully, passed my exams, and attended all the required lectures. I have sown compassion and love with thousands around the globe. I have been called a doctor and minister almost my entire life. I have always possessed a special healing touch. Following what I felt, was more important than doing what was expected. I felt and honored the deep penetrating urge of Spirit.

I really tried to be someone different for many years; to please my parents, my two ex-husbands and so on. Spirit never left me alone for very long, even as I attended various churches looking for something I could not find there, outside of me. It is always on the inside of us!

People tell me I'm Positive; I'm Powerful and a Natural Healer. That is absolutely wonderful. Yet, I am faced with having to <u>feel</u> it, to proclaim it for myself. Not in an egoistical nor arrogant way. I must truly <u>feel</u> my Power in my heart, know it deeply, comprehend it completely and live it lovingly.

My preparation is complete. God has blessed me with strength, tenacity, courage, wisdom, and understanding. I express Love, Compassion and Peace everywhere I AM.

What is your Purpose? YOU get to name it and define it!

Just remember:

When God leads… just follow!

Websites of those referenced:

Ahimki Center for Wholeness/Dr. Mark Armstrong – www.ahimki.net

Darryl Hood – email: darrylhood@hotmail.com

Don Miguel Ruiz – www.miguelruiz.com

Dr. Pamelaia Sanders – www.pamelaia.com

Dr. Vanessa McAdams-Mahmoud/Mandala Psychotherapy – www.vanessamahmoud.net

Gentleman Jim – www.gentlemanjim5944.net

Karen..Bishop   www.whatsuponplanetearth.com

Marlo Oliver –..www.lifeafterbreath.com

Raja Crumbly – www.rajaiam.com

Rickie Byars-Beckwith – www.agapelive.com

Sandy Rodgers – www.sandyrodgersministries.org

The Secret – www.thesecret.tv

William Saafir – www.williamsaafir.webs.com

Sandy Rodgers

Bio

Sandy Rodgers: Published Author, Skilled Speaker, Compassionate Educator, Inspires Change by Empowering People. Her name means "Defender of Mankind," and she has dedicated her life in service to others; serving as a social service advocate and human justice activist. She willing serves all of humanity, children, elders, men, women and those infirmed by disabilities. Sandy helps to release people from the prison of their minds and thoughts to become the person they are capable of being.

Sandy's business education began with a family collaborative called 'Unity-N-Business'. She received "Outstanding Young Women Of America" and "Who's Who In The West" awards for her unselfish contributions to her community. Sandy has received many awards, accolades and been honored by several organizations in Los Angeles including proclamations from the Mayor, Council members and City of Los Angeles; and in Atlanta inclusion in the Tenth Anniversary edition of "Who's Who In Black Atlanta", 2007 International Peace Award, among others.

Sandy opened Nu Vision Modeling and Entertainment Inc, in South Central Los Angeles. Several goals were achieved, the most significant was the fact that 100% of all graduating seniors attended a school of higher learning after graduation, due to her influence and the impact the training had on the young people. She recognized a lack of self-esteem and self- love often led to destructive lifestyles for many youngsters living in the inner city. She served as co-sponsor for the 1993 USA-Berlin Initiative, an exchange program that brought together a wide range of ethnic backgrounds for one common goal, to leave a legacy of peace in Los Angeles.

Sandy is a National Motivational Speaker for such organizations as NABNA -National Association of Black Narcotic Agents; Southwest Los Angeles College in California and The African American Summit for Peace, Justice and Equality in Fort Worth, Texas. Sandy is excited to speak to youth groups especially those in youth detention centers. She often speaks at Women's Conferences nationally.

She is the author of several books and collaborates with celebrities in telling their stories.
She has established several training companies, two of which are Keep America Strong and Glasgow Armstead Behavioral Group whose goals are to improve the lives of individuals and to assist with the development of communities across the nation.

CELEBRATE
© Sandy Rodgers Ministries

Norman Vincent Peale writes in his book, "The Power of Positive Thinking" 'throw your heart over the bar and your body will follow'. Another example I read is 'A little axe can cut down a large tree' a Jamaican proverb.

For today give full attention to exactly what you desire to achieve. This means to be very precise and crystal clear about your intentions, expectations and goals. What do you really want to manifest? Why?

As you sit today giving Thanks for the past year and all the wonderful opportunities you created, think beyond your comfort zone and decide what it is you want to accomplish for this year.

Once you have the clear, vivid image in your thoughts, go ahead and put your whole heart (emotions) into manifesting it. Do this expecting the best with each thought, repetition is crucial. Affirm as often as possible throughout each hour, "**I DESERVE MY DREAM!**"

As with the axe, it refers to Faith. With just a small amount of Faith you can knock down and cut down any tree of fear, doubt and/or worry. If you need help, call upon your Axe Angels to help! The Axe Angels are those friends and family members who totally believe in you, especially at times when you may wonder about yourself.

Today, celebrate your life. Give Thanks for who you are currently and who you are creating. You are so much more than you have ever thought or imagined. **Throw Your Heart Over The Bar** and your body will follow!

I congratulate you on achieving Tremendous Success this year!!!

Celebrate your victory today. Have a Grand Party. See the audience; hear the applause as you receive your Prize of Victory.

You, my dear, ARE VICTORIOUS.